THE LATER WORK OF TITIAN

THE LATER WORK OF TITIAN

CLAUDE PHILLIPS

Keeper of the Wallace Collection

CRESCENT MOON

First published 1898. This edition © 2017.

Printed and bound in the U.S.A.
Set in Book Antiqua 10 on 14pt.
Designed by Radiance Graphics.

British Library Cataloguing in Publication data

ISBN-13 9781861716637

CRESCENT MOON PUBLISHING
P.O. Box 1312, Maidstone, Kent, ME14 5XU
Great Britain, www.crmoon.com

CONTENTS

NOTE ON THE TEXT

The text is from *The Later Work of Titian* by Claude Phillips, 1898.

Footnotes are in square brackets, thus: [*1]

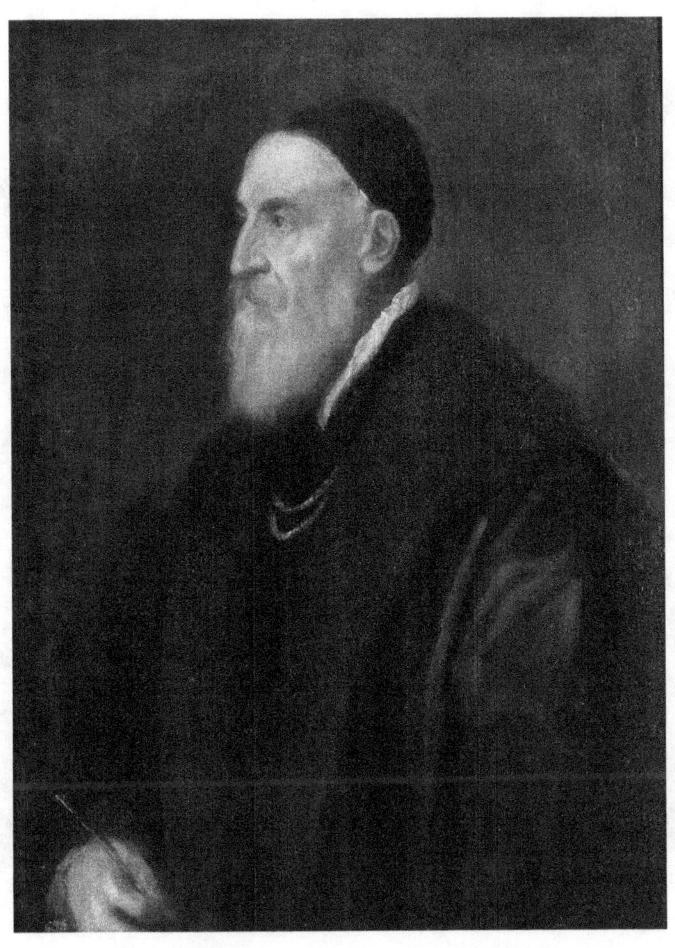

Titian, Self-Portrait, 1565, Prado, Madrid

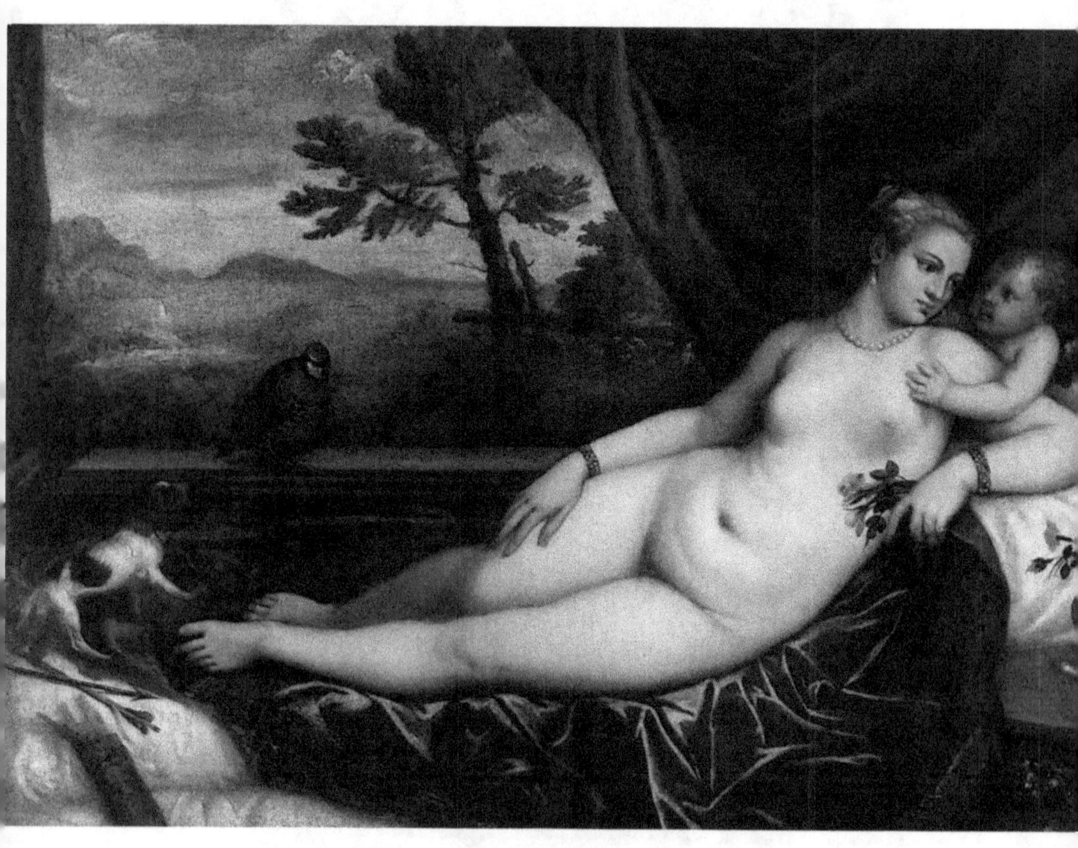

Titian, Venus and Cupid, 1550, Uffizi

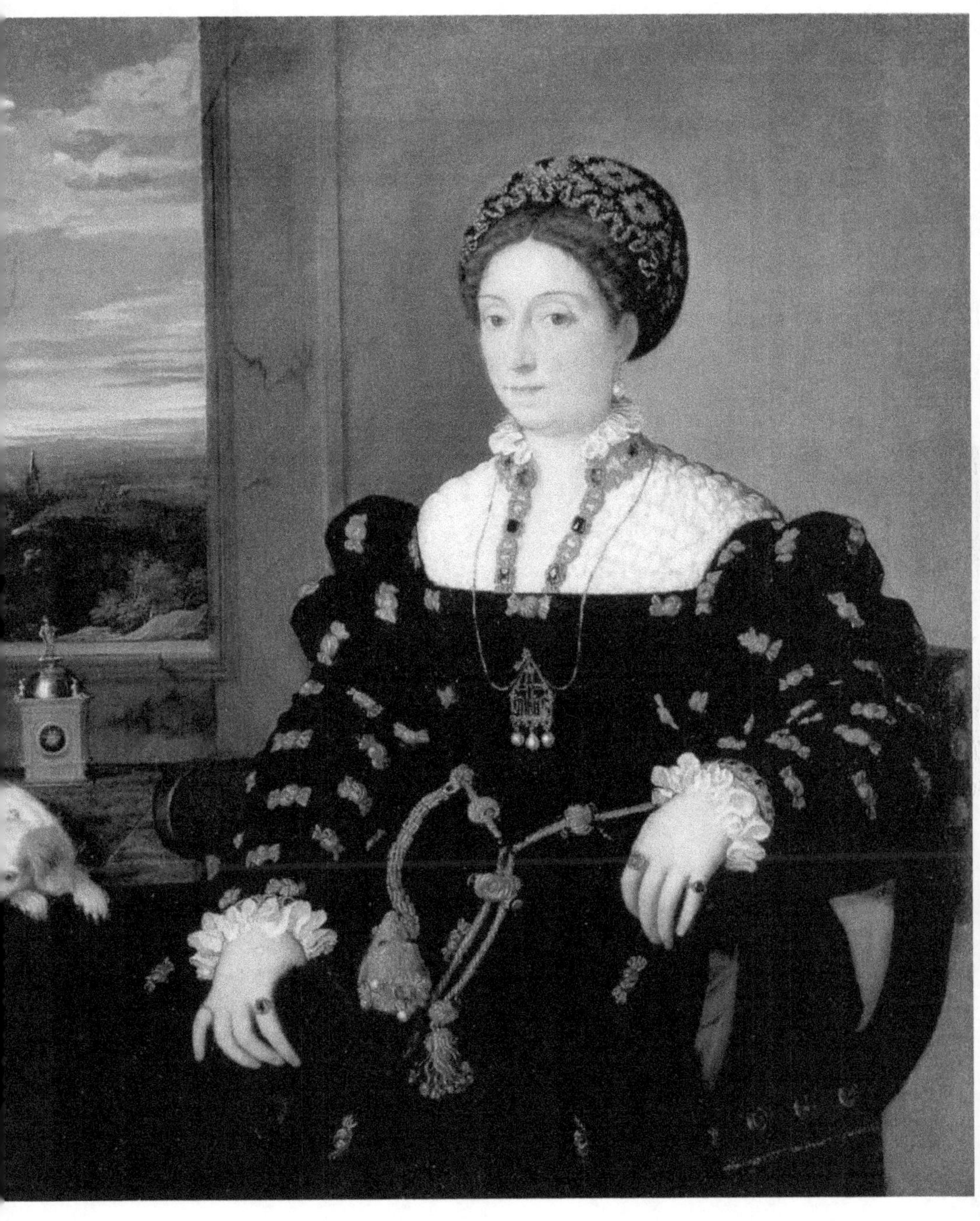

Titian, Portrait of Eleonora Gonzaga, 1538, Uffizi

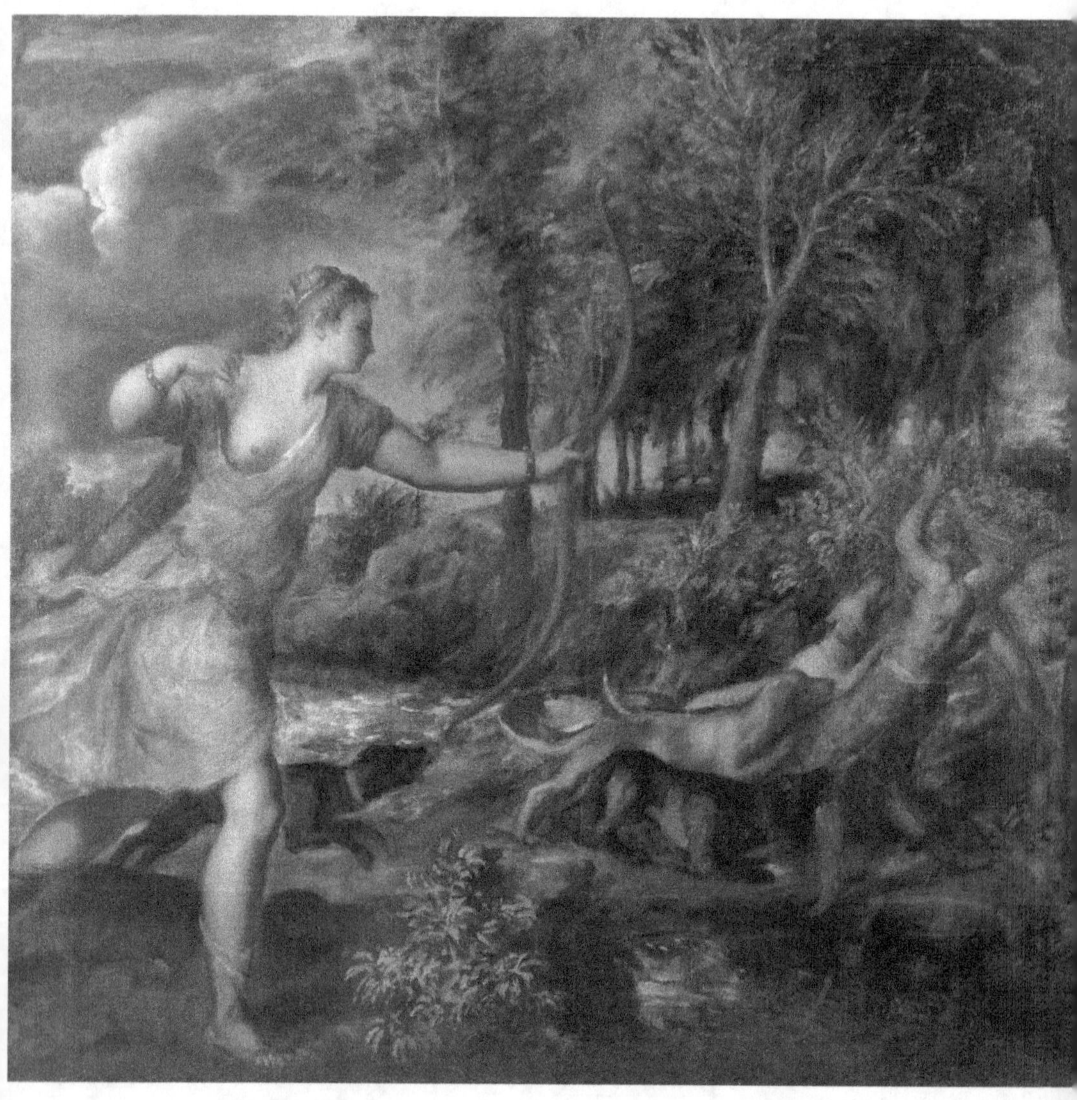

Titian, The Death of Actaeon 1559-75
National Gallery, London

CHAPTER I

Having followed Titian as far as the year 1530, rendered memorable by that sensational, and, of its kind, triumphant achievement, *The Martyrdom of St. Peter the Dominican*, we must retrace our steps some three years in order to dwell a little upon an incident which must appear of vital importance to those who seek to understand Titian's life, and, above all, to follow the development of his art during the middle period of splendid maturity reaching to the confines of old age. This incident is the meeting with Pietro Aretino at Venice in 1527, and the gradual strengthening by mutual service and mutual inclination of the bonds of a friendship which is to endure without break until the life of the Aretine comes, many years later, to a sudden and violent end. Titian was at that time fifty years of age, and he might thus be deemed to have over-passed the age of sensuous delights. Yet it must be remembered that he was in the fullest vigour of manhood, and had only then arrived at the middle point of a career which, in its untroubled serenity, was to endure for a full half-century more, less a single year. Three years later on, that is to say in the middle of August 1530, the death of his wife Cecilia, who had borne to him Pomponio, Orazio, and Lavinia, left him all disconsolate, and so embarrassed with the cares of his young family that he was compelled to appeal to his sister Orsa, who thereupon came from Cadore to preside over his household. The highest point of celebrity, of favour with princes and magnates, having been attained, and a certain royalty in Venetian art being already conceded to him, there was no longer any obstacle to the organising of a life in which all the refinements of culture and all the delights of sense were to form the most agreeable relief to days of continuous and magnificently fruitful labour. It is just because Titian's art of this great period of some twenty years so entirely accords with what we know, and may legitimately infer, to have been his life at this time, that it becomes important to consider the friendship with Aretino and the rise of the so-called Triumvirate, which was a kind of Council of Three, having as its *raison d'être* the mutual furtherance of material interests, and the pursuit of art, love, and pleasure. The third member of the Triumvirate was Jacopo Tatti or del Sansovino, the Florentine sculptor, whose fame and fortune were so far above his deserts as an artist. Coming to Venice after the sack of Rome, which so entirely for the moment disorganised art and artists in the pontifical city, he elected to remain there notwithstanding the pressing invitations sent to him by Francis the First to take service with him. In 1529 he was appointed architect of San Marco, and he then by his adhesion completed the Triumvirate which was to endure for more than a quarter of a century.

It has always excited a certain sense of distrust in Titian, and caused the world to form a lower estimate of his character than it would otherwise have done, that he should have been capable of thus living in the closest and most fraternal intimacy with a man so spotted and in many ways so infamous as Aretino. Without precisely calling Titian to account in set terms, his biographers Crowe and Cavalcaselle, and above all M. Georges Lafenestre in *La Vie et L'Oeuvre du Titien*, have relentlessly raked up Aretino's past before he came together with the Cadorine, and as pitilessly laid bare that organised system of professional sycophancy, adulation, scurrilous libel, and blackmail, which was the foundation and the backbone of his life of outward pomp and luxurious ease at Venice. By them, as by his other biographers, he has been judged, not indeed unjustly, yet perhaps too much from the standard of our own time, too little from that of his own. With all his infamies, Aretino was a man whom sovereigns and princes, nay even pontiffs, delighted to honour, or rather to distinguish by honours. The Marquess Federigo Gonzaga of Mantua, the Duke Guidobaldo II. of Urbino, among many others, showed themselves ready to propitiate him; and such a man as Titian the worldly-wise, the lover of splendid living to whom ample means and the fruitful favour of the great were a necessity; who was grasping yet not avaricious, who loved wealth chiefly because it secured material consideration and a life of serene enjoyment; such a man could not be expected to rise superior to the temptations presented by a friendship with Aretino, or to despise the immense advantages which it included. As he is revealed by his biographers, and above all by himself, Aretino was essentially "good company." He could pass off his most flagrant misdeeds, his worst sallies, with a certain large and Rabelaisian gaiety; if he made money his chief god, it was to spend it in magnificent clothes and high living, but also at times with an intelligent and even a beneficent liberality. He was a fine though not an unerring connoisseur of art, he had a passionate love of music, and an unusually exquisite perception of the beauties of Nature.

To hint that the lower nature of the man corrupted that of Titian, and exercised a disintegrating influence over his art, would be to go far beyond the requirements of the case. The great

Venetian, though he might at this stage be much nearer to earth than in those early days when he was enveloped in the golden glow of Giorgione's overmastering influence, could never have lowered himself to the level of those too famous *Sonetti Lussuriosi* which brought down the vengeance of even a Medici Pope (Clement VII.) upon Aretino the writer, Giulio Romano the illustrator, and Marcantonio Raimondi the engraver. Gracious and dignified in sensuousness he always remained even when, as at this middle stage of his career, the vivifying shafts of poetry no longer pierced through, and transmuted with their vibration of true passion, the fair realities of life. He could never have been guilty of the frigid and calculated indecency of a Giulio Romano; he could not have cast aside all conventional restraints, of taste as well as of propriety, as Rubens and even Rembrandt did on occasion; but as Van Dyck, the child of Titian almost as much as he was the child of Rubens, ever shrank from doing. Still the ease and splendour of the life at Biri Grande – that pleasant abode with its fair gardens overlooking Murano, the Lagoons, and the Friulan Alps, to which Titian migrated in 1531 – the Epicureanism which saturated the atmosphere, the necessity for keeping constantly in view the material side of life, all these things operated to colour the creations which mark this period of Titian's practice, at which he has reached the apex of pictorial achievement, but shows himself too serene in sensuousness, too unruffled in the masterly practice of his profession to give to the heart the absolute satisfaction that he affords to the eyes. This is the greatest test of genius of the first order – to preserve undimmed in mature manhood and old age the gift of imaginative interpretation which youth and love give, or lend, to so many who, buoyed up by momentary inspiration, are yet not to remain permanently in the first rank. With Titian at this time supreme ability is not invariably illumined from within by the lamp of genius; the light flashes forth nevertheless, now and again, and most often in those portraits of men of which the sublime *Charles V. at Mühlberg* is the greatest. Towards the end the flame will rise once more and steadily burn, with something on occasion of the old heat, but with a hue paler and more mysterious, such as may naturally be the outward symbol of genius on the confines of eternity.

The second period, following upon the completion of the *St. Peter Martyr,* is one less of great altar-pieces and *poesie* such as the miscalled *Sacred and Profane Love* (*Medea and Venus*), the *Bacchanals,* and the *Bacchus and Ariadne,* than it is of splendid nudities and great portraits. In the former, however mythological be the subject, it is generally chosen but to afford a decent pretext for the generous display of beauty unveiled. The portraits are at this stage less often intimate and soul-searching in their summing up of a human personality than they are official presentments of great personages and noble dames; showing them, no doubt, without false adulation or cheap idealisation, yet much as they desire to appear to their allies, their friends, and their subjects, sovereign in natural dignity and aristocratic grace, yet essentially in a moment of representation. Farther on the great altar-pieces reappear more sombre, more agitated in passion, as befits the period of the sixteenth century in which Titian's latest years are passed, and the patrons for whom he paints. Of the *poesie* there is then a new upspringing, a new efflorescence, and we get by the side of the *Venus and Adonis,* the *Diana and Actæon,* the *Diana and Calisto,* the *Rape of Europa,* such pieces of a more exquisite and penetrating poetry as the *Venere del Pardo* of Paris, and the *Nymph and Shepherd* of Vienna.

This appears to be the right place to say a word about the magnificent engraving by Van Dalen of a portrait, no longer known to exist, but which has, upon the evidence apparently of the print, been put down as that of Titian by himself. It represents a bearded man of some thirty-five years, dressed in a rich but sombre habit, and holding a book. The portrait is evidently not that of a painter by himself, nor does it represent Titian at any age; but it finely suggests, even in black and white, a noble original by the master. Now, a comparison with the best authenticated portrait of Aretino, the superb three-quarter length painted in 1545, and actually at the Pitti Palace, reveals certain marked similarities of feature and type, notwithstanding the very considerable difference of age between the personages represented. Very striking is the agreement of eye and nose in either case, while in the younger as in the older man we note an idiosyncrasy in which vigorous intellect as well as strong sensuality has full play. Van Dalen's engraving very probably reproduces one of the lost portraits of Aretino by Titian. In Crowe and Cavalcaselle's *Biography* (vol. i. pp. 317-319) we learn from correspondence interchanged in the summer of 1527 between Federigo Gonzaga, Titian, and Aretino, that the painter, in order to propitiate the Mantuan ruler, sent to him with a letter, the exaggerated flattery of which savours of Aretino's precept and example, portraits of the latter and of Signor Hieronimo Adorno, another "faithful servant" of the Marquess. Now Aretino was born in 1492, so that in 1527 he would be thirty-five, which appears to be just about the age of the vigorous and splendid personage in Van Dalen's print.

Some reasons were given in the former section of this monograph[*1] for the assertion that the *Madonna with St. Catherine*, mentioned in a letter from Giacomo Malatesta to the Marchese Federigo Gonzaga, dated February 1530, was not, as is assumed by Crowe and Cavalcaselle, the *Madonna del Coniglio* of the Louvre, but the *Madonna and Child with St. John the Baptist and St. Catherine*, which is No. 635 at the National Gallery.[*2] Few pictures of the master have been more frequently copied and adapted than this radiantly beautiful piece, in which the dominant chord of the scheme of colour is composed by the cerulean blues of the heavens and the Virgin's entire dress, the deep luscious greens of the landscape, and the peculiar, pale, citron hue, relieved with a crimson girdle, of the robe worn by the St. Catherine, a splendid Venetian beauty of no very refined type or emotional intensity. Perfect repose and serenity are the keynote of the conception, which in its luxuriant beauty has little of the power to touch that must be conceded to the more naïve and equally splendid *Madonna del Coniglio*.[*3] It is above all in the wonderful Venetian landscape – a mountain-bordered vale, along which flocks and herds are being driven, under a sky of the most intense blue – that the master shows himself supreme. Nature is therein not so much detailed as synthesised with a sweeping breadth which makes of the scene not the reflection of one beautiful spot in the Venetian territory, but without loss of essential truth or character a very type of Venetian landscape of the sixteenth century. These herdsmen and their flocks, and also the note of warning in the sky of supernatural splendour, recall the beautiful Venetian storm-landscape in the royal collection at Buckingham Palace. This has been very generally attributed to Titian himself,[*4] and described as the only canvas still extant in which he has made landscape his one and only theme. It has, indeed, a rare and mysterious power to move, a true poetry of interpretation. A fleeting moment, full of portent as well as of beauty, has been seized; the smile traversed by a frown of the stormy sky, half overshadowing half revealing the wooded slopes, the rich plain, and the distant mountains, is rendered with a rare felicity. The beauty is, all the same, in the conception and in the thing actually seen – much less in the actual painting. It is hardly possible to convince oneself, comparing the work with such landscape backgrounds as those in this picture at the National Gallery in the somewhat earlier *Madonna del Coniglio*, and the gigantic *St. Peter Martyr*, or, indeed, in a score of other genuine productions, that the depth, the vigour, the authority of Titian himself are here to be recognised. The weak treatment of the great Titianesque tree in the foreground, with its too summarily indicated foliage – to select only one detail that comes naturally to hand – would in itself suffice to bring such an attribution into question.

Vasari states, speaking confessedly from hearsay, that in 1530, the Emperor Charles V. being at Bologna, Titian was summoned thither by Cardinal Ippolito de' Medici, using Aretino as an intermediary, and that he on that occasion executed a most admirable portrait of His Majesty, all in arms, which had so much success that the artist received as a present a thousand scudi. Crowe and Cavalcaselle, however, adduce strong evidence to prove that Titian was busy in Venice for Federigo Gonzaga at the time of the Emperor's first visit, and that he only proceeded to Bologna in July to paint for the Marquess of Mantua the portrait of a Bolognese beauty, *La Cornelia*, the lady-in-waiting of the Countess Pepoli, whom Covas, the all-powerful political secretary of Charles the Fifth, had seen and admired at the splendid entertainments given by the Pepoli to the Emperor. Vasari has in all probability confounded this journey of Charles in 1530 with that subsequent one undertaken in 1532 when Titian not only portrayed the Emperor, but also painted an admirable likeness of Ippolito de' Medici presently to be described. He had the bad luck on this occasion to miss the lady Cornelia, who had retired to Nuvolara, indisposed and not in good face. The letter written by our painter to the Marquess in connection with this incident[*5] is chiefly remarkable as affording evidence of his too great anxiety to portray the lady without approaching her, relying merely on the portrait, "che fece quel altro pittore della detta Cornelia"; of his unwillingness to proceed to Nuvolara, unless the picture thus done at second hand should require alteration. In truth we have lighted here upon one of Titian's most besetting sins, this willingness, this eagerness, when occasion offers, to paint portraits without direct reference to the model. In this connection we are reminded that he never saw Francis the First, whose likeness he notwithstanding painted with so showy and superficial a magnificence as to make up to the casual observer for the absence of true vitality;[*6] that the Empress Isabella, Charles V.'s consort, when at the behest of the monarch he produced her sumptuous but lifeless and empty portrait, now in the great gallery of the Prado, was long since dead. He consented, basing his picture upon a likeness of much earlier date, to paint Isabella d'Este Gonzaga as a young woman when she was already an old one, thereby flattering an amiable and natural weakness in this great princess and unrivalled dilettante, but impairing his own position as an artist of supreme rank.[*7] It is not necessary to include in this category the popular *Caterina Cornaro* of the Uffizi, since it is confessedly nothing but a fancy portrait, making no reference to the true aspect at any period of the long-since deceased queen of Cyprus, and, what is more, no original Titian, but at the utmost an atelier piece from his *entourage*. Take, however, as an instance the *Francis the First*, which was painted some few years later than the time at which we have now arrived, and at about the same period as the *Isabella d'Este*. Though as a *portrait d'apparat* it makes its effect, and reveals the sovereign accomplishment of the master, does it not shrink into the merest insignificance when compared with such renderings from life as the successive portraits of *Charles the Fifth*, the *Ippolito de' Medici*, the *Francesco Maria della Rovere*? This is as it must and should be, and Titian is not the less great, but the greater, because he cannot convincingly evolve at second hand the true human individuality, physical and mental, of man or woman.

It was in the earlier part of 1531 that Titian painted for Federigo Gonzaga a *St. Jerome* and a *St. Mary Magdalene*, destined for the famous Vittoria Colonna, Marchioness of Pescara, who had expressed to the ruler of Mantua the desire to possess such a picture. Gonzaga writes to the Marchioness on March 11, 1831[*8]: – "Ho subito mandate a Venezia e scritto a Titiano, quale è forse il piu eccellente in quell' arte che a nostri tempi si ritrovi, ed è tutto mio, ricercandolo con grande instantia a volerne fare una bella lagrimosa piu che si so puo, e farmela haver presto." The passage is worth quoting as showing the estimation in which Titian was held at a court which had known and still knew the greatest Italian masters of the art.

It is not possible at present to identify with any extant painting the *St. Jerome*, of which we know that it hung in the private apartments of the Marchioness Isabella at Mantua. The writer is unable to accept Crowe and Cavalcaselle's suggestion that it may be the fine moonlight landscape with St. Jerome in prayer which is now in the Long Gallery of the Louvre. This piece, if indeed it be by Titian, which is by no means certain, must belong to his late time. The landscape, which is marked by a beautiful and wholly unconventional treatment of moonlight, for which it would not be easy to find a parallel in the painting of the time, is worthy of the Cadorine, and agrees well, especially in the broad treatment of foliage, with, for instance, the background in the late *Venus and Cupid* of the Tribuna.[*9] The figure of St. Jerome, on the other hand, does not in the peculiar tightness of the modelling, or in the flesh-tints, recall Titian's masterly synthetic way of going to work in works of this late period. The noble *St. Jerome* of the Brera, which indubitably belongs to a well-advanced stage in the late time, will be dealt with in its right place. Though it does not appear probable that we have, in the much-admired *Magdalen* of the Pitti, the picture here referred to – this last having belonged to Francesco Maria della Rovere, Duke of Urbino, and representing, to judge by style, a somewhat more advanced period in the painter's career – it may be convenient to mention it here. As an example of accomplished brush-work, of handling careful and yet splendid in breadth, it is indeed worthy of all admiration. The colours of the fair human body, the marvellous wealth of golden blond hair, the youthful flesh glowing semi-transparent, and suggesting the rush of the blood beneath; these are also the colours of the picture, aided only by the indefinite landscape and the deep blue sky of the background. If this were to be accepted as the *Magdalen* painted for Federigo Gonzaga, we must hold, nevertheless, that Titian with his masterpiece of painting only half satisfied the requirements of his patron. *Bellissima* this Magdalen undoubtedly is, but hardly *lagrimosa pin che si puo.* She is a *belle pécheresse* whose repentance sits all too lightly upon her, whose consciousness of a physical charm not easily to be withstood is hardly disguised. Somehow, although the picture in no way oversteps the bounds of decency, and cannot be objected to even by the most over-scrupulous, there is latent in it a jarring note of unrefinement in the presentment of exuberant youth and beauty which we do not find in the more avowedly sensuous *Venus of the Tribuna*. This last is an avowed act of worship by the artist of the naked human body, and as such, in its noble frankness, free from all offence, except to those whose scruples in matters of art we are not here called upon to consider. From this *Magdalen* to that much later one of the Hermitage, which will be described farther on, is a great step upwards, and it is a step which, in passing from the middle to the last period, we shall more than once find ourselves taking.

It is impossible to give even in outline here an account of Titian's correspondence and business relations with his noble and royal patrons, instructive as it is to follow these out, and to see how, under the influence of Aretino, his natural eagerness to grasp in every direction at material advantages is sharpened; how he becomes at once more humble and more pressing, covering with the manner and the tone appropriate to courts the reiterated demands of the keen and indefatigable man of business. It is the less necessary to attempt any such account in these pages – dealing as we are chiefly with the work and not primarily with the life of Titian – seeing that in Crowe and Cavalcaselle's admirable biography this side of the subject, among many others, is most patiently and exhaustively dealt with.

In 1531 we read of a *Boy Baptist* by Titian sent by Aretino to Maximian Stampa, an imperialist partisan in command of the castle of Milan. The donor particularly dwells upon "the beautiful curl of the Baptist's hair, the fairness of his skin, etc.," a description which recalls to us, in striking fashion, the little St. John in the *Virgin and Child with St. Catherine* of the National Gallery, which belongs, as has been shown, to the same time.

It was on the occasion of the second visit of the Emperor and his court to Bologna at the close of 1532 that Titian first came in personal contact with Charles V., and obtained from that monarch his first sitting. In the course of an inspection, with Federigo Gonzaga himself as cicerone, of the art treasures preserved in the palace at Mantua, the Emperor saw the portrait by Titian of

Federigo, and was so much struck with it, so intent upon obtaining a portrait of himself from the same brush, that the Marquess wrote off at once pressing our master to join him without delay in his capital. Titian preferred, however, to go direct to Bologna in the train of his earlier patron Alfonso d'Este. It was on this occasion that Charles's all-powerful secretary, the greedy, overbearing Covos, exacted as a gift from the agents of the Duke of Ferrara, among other things, a portrait of Alfonso himself by Titian; and in all probability obtained also a portrait from the same hand of Ercole d'Este, the heir-apparent. There is evidence to show that the portrait of Alfonso was at once handed over to, or appropriated by, the Emperor.

Whether this was the picture described by Vasari as representing the prince with his arm resting on a great piece of artillery, does not appear. Of this last a copy exists in the Pitti Gallery which Crowe and Cavalcaselle have ascribed to Dosso Dossi, but the original is nowhere to be traced. The Ferrarese ruler is, in this last canvas, depicted as a man of forty or upwards, of resolute and somewhat careworn aspect. It has already been demonstrated, on evidence furnished by Herr Carl Justi, that the supposed portrait of Alfonso, in the gallery of the Prado at Madrid, cannot possibly represent Titian's patron at any stage of his career, but in all probability, like the so-called *Giorgio Cornaro* of Castle Howard, is a likeness of his son and successor, Ercole II.

Titian's first portrait of the Emperor, a full-length in which he appeared in armour with a generalissimo's baton of command, was taken in 1556 from Brussels to Madrid, after the formal ceremony of abdication, and perished, it would appear, in one of the too numerous fires which have devastated from time to time the royal palaces of the Spanish capital and its neighbourhood. To the same period belongs, no doubt, the noble full-length of Charles in gala court costume which now hangs in the *Sala de la Reina Isabel* in the Prado Gallery, as a pendant to Titian's portrait of Philip II. in youth. Crowe and Cavalcaselle assume that not this picture, but a replica, was the one which found its way into

Charles I.'s collection, and was there catalogued by Van der Doort as "the Emperor Charles the Fifth, brought by the king from Spain, being done at length with a big white Irish dog" – going afterwards, at the dispersal of the king's effects, to Sir Balthasar Gerbier for £150. There is, however, no valid reason for doubting that this is the very picture owned for a time by Charles I., and which busy intriguing Gerbier afterwards bought, only to part with it to Cardenas the Spanish ambassador.[*10] Other famous originals by Titian were among the choicest gifts made by Philip IV. to Prince Charles at the time of his runaway expedition to Madrid with the Duke of Buckingham, and this was no doubt among them. Confirmation is supplied by the fact that the references to the existence of this picture in the royal palaces of Madrid are for the reigns of Philip II., Charles II., and Charles III., thus leaving a large gap unaccounted for. Dimmed as the great portrait is, robbed of its glow and its chastened splendour in a variety of ways, it is still a rare example of the master's unequalled power in rendering race, the unaffected consciousness of exalted rank, natural as distinguished from assumed dignity. There is here no demonstrative assertion of *grandeza*, no menacing display of truculent authority, but an absolutely serene and simple attitude such as can only be the outcome of a consciousness of supreme rank and responsibility which it can never have occurred to any one to call into question. To see and perpetuate these subtle qualities, which go so far to redeem the physical drawbacks of the House of Hapsburg, the painter must have had a peculiar instinct for what is aristocratic in the higher sense of the word – that is, both outwardly and inwardly distinguished. This was indeed one of the leading characteristics of Titian's great art, more especially in portraiture. Giorgione went deeper, knowing the secret of the soul's refinement, the aristocracy of poetry and passion; Lotto sympathetically laid bare the heart's secrets and showed the pathetic helplessness of humanity. Tintoretto communicated his own savage grandeur, his own unrest, to those whom he depicted; Paolo Veronese charmed without *arrière-pensée* by the intensity of vitality which with perfect simplicity he preserved in his sitters. Yet to Titian must be conceded absolute supremacy in the rendering not only of the outward but of the essential dignity, the refinement of type and bearing, which without doubt come unconsciously to those who can boast a noble and illustrious ancestry.

Again the writer hesitates to agree with Crowe and Cavalcaselle when they place at this period, that is to say about 1533, the superb *Allegory* of the Louvre (No. 1589), which is very generally believed to represent the famous commander Alfonso d'Avalos, Marqués del Vasto, with his family. The eminent biographers of Titian connect the picture with the return of d'Avalos from the campaign against the Turks, undertaken by him in the autumn of 1532, under the leadership of Croy, at the behest of his imperial master. They hazard the surmise that the picture, though painted after Alfonso's return, symbolises his departure for the wars, "consoled by Victory, Love, and Hymen." A more natural conclusion would surely be that what Titian has sought to suggest is the return of the commander to enjoy the hard-earned fruits of victory.

The Italo-Spanish grandee was born at Naples in 1502, so that at this date he would have been but thirty-one years of age, whereas the mailed warrior of the *Allegory* is at least forty, perhaps older. Moreover, and this is the essential point, the technical qualities of the picture, the wonderful easy mastery of the handling, the peculiarities of the colouring and the general tone, surely point to a rather later date, to a period, indeed, some ten years ahead of the time at which we have arrived. If we are to accept the tradition that this Allegory, or quasi-allegorical portrait-piece, giving a fanciful embodiment to the pleasures of martial domination, of conjugal love, of well-earned peace and plenty, represents d'Avalos, his consort Mary of Arragon, and their family – and a comparison with the well-authenticated portrait of Del Vasto in the *Allocution* of Madrid does not carry with it entire conviction – we must perforce place the Louvre picture some ten years later than do Crowe and Cavalcaselle. Apart from the question of identification, it appears to the writer that the technical execution of the piece would lead to a similar conclusion.[*11]

To this year, 1533, belongs one of the masterpieces in portraiture of our painter, the wonderful *Cardinal Ippolito de' Medici in a Hungarian habit* of the Pitti. This youthful Prince of the Church, the natural son of Giuliano de' Medici, Duke of Nemours, was born in 1511, so that when Titian so incomparably portrayed him, he was, for all the perfect maturity of his virile beauty, for all the perfect self-possession of his aspect, but twenty-two years of age. He was the passionate worshipper of the divine Giulia Gonzaga, whose portrait he caused to be painted by Sebastiano del Piombo. His part in the war undertaken by Charles V. in 1532, against the Turks, had been a strange one. Clement VII., his relative, had appointed him Legate and sent him to Vienna at the head of three hundred musketeers. But when Charles withdrew from the army to return to Italy, the Italian contingent, instead of going in pursuit of the Sultan into Hungary, opportunely mutinied, thus affording to their pleasure-loving leader the desired pretext for riding back with them through the Austrian provinces, with eyes wilfully closed the while to their acts of depredation. It was in the rich and fantastic habit of a Hungarian captain that the handsome young Medici was now painted by Titian at Bologna, the result being a portrait unique of its kind even in his life-work. The sombre glow of the supple, youthful flesh, the red-brown of the rich velvet habit which defines the perfect shape of Ippolito, the red of the fantastic plumed head-dress worn by him with such sovereign ease, make up a deep harmony, warm, yet not in the technical sense hot, and of indescribable effect. And this effect is centralised in the uncanny glance, the mysterious aspect of the man whom, as we see him here, a woman might love for his beauty, but a man would do well to distrust. The smaller portrait painted by Titian about the same time of the young Cardinal fully armed – the one which, with the Pitti picture, Vasari saw in the closet (*guardaroba*) of

Cosimo, Duke of Tuscany – is not now known to exist.[*12]

It may be convenient to mention here one of the most magnificent among the male portraits of Titian, the *Young Nobleman* in the Sala di Marte of the Pitti Gallery, although its exact place in the middle time of the artist it is, failing all data on the point, not easy to determine. At Florence there has somehow been attached to it the curious name *Howard duca di Norfolk*,[*13] but upon what grounds, if any, the writer is unable to state. The master of Cadore never painted a head more finely or with a more exquisite finesse, never more happily characterised a face, than that of this resolute, self-contained young patrician with the curly chestnut hair and the short, fine beard and moustache – a personage high of rank, doubtless, notwithstanding the studied simplicity of his dress. Because we know nothing of the sitter, and there is in his pose and general aspect nothing sensational, this masterpiece is, if not precisely not less celebrated among connoisseurs, at any rate less popular with the larger public, than it deserves to be.[*14]

The noble altar-piece in the church of S. Giovanni Elemosinario at Venice showing the saint of that name enthroned, and giving alms to a beggar, belongs to the close of 1533 or thereabouts, since the high-altar was finished in the month of October of that year. According to Vasari, it must be regarded as having served above all to assert once for all the supremacy of Titian over Pordenone, whose friends had obtained for him the commission to paint in competition with the Cadorine an altar-piece for one of the apsidal chapels of the church, where, indeed, his work is still to be seen.[*15] Titian's canvas, like most of the great altar-pieces of the middle time, was originally arched at the top; but the vandalism of a subsequent epoch has, as in the case of the *Madonna di S. Niccola*, now in the Vatican, made of this arch a square, thereby greatly impairing the majesty of the general effect. Titian here solves the problem of combining the strong and simple decorative aspect demanded by the position of the work as the central feature of a small church, with the utmost pathos and dignity, thus doing incomparably in his own way – the way of the colourist and the warm, the essentially human realist – what Michelangelo had, soaring high above earth, accomplished with unapproachable sublimity in the *Prophets* and *Sibyls* of the Sixtine Chapel.

The colour is appropriately sober, yet a general tone is produced of great strength and astonishing effectiveness. The illumination is that of the open air, tempered and modified by an overhanging canopy of green; the great effect is obtained by the brilliant grayish white of the saint's alb, dominating and keeping in due balance the red of the rochet and the under-robes, the cloud-veiled sky, the marble throne or podium, the dark green hanging. This picture must have had in the years to follow a strong and lasting influence on Paolo Veronese, the keynote to whose audaciously brilliant yet never over-dazzling colour is this use of white and gray in large dominating masses. The noble figure of S. Giovanni gave him a prototype for many of his imposing figures of bearded old men. There is a strong reminiscence, too, of the saint's attitude in one of the most wonderful of extant Veroneses – that sumptuous altar-piece *SS. Anthony, Cornelius, and Cyprian with a Page*, in the Brera, for which he invented a harmony as delicious as it is daring, composed wholly of violet-purple, green, and gold.

CHAPTER II

Within the years 1532 and 1538, or thereabouts, would appear to fall Titian's relations with another princely patron, Francesco Maria della Rovere, Duke of Urbino, the nephew of the redoubtable Pope Julius II., whose qualities of martial ardour and unbridled passion he reproduced in an exaggerated form. By his mother, Giovanna da Montefeltro, he descended also from the rightful dynasty of Urbino, to which he succeeded in virtue of adoption. His life of perpetual strife, of warfare in defence of his more than once lost and reconquered duchy, and as the captain first of the army of the Church, afterwards of the Venetian forces, came to an abrupt end in 1538. With his own hand he had, in the ardent days of his youth, slain in the open streets of Ravenna the handsome, sinister Cardinal Alidosi, thereby bringing down upon himself the anathemas of his uncle, Julius II., and furnishing to his successor, the Medici pope Leo X., the best possible excuse for the sequestration of the duchy of Urbino in favour of his own house. He himself died by poison, suspicion resting upon the infamous Pier Luigi Farnese, the son of Paul III.

Francesco Maria had espoused Eleonora Gonzaga, the sister of Titian's protector, Federigo, and it is probably through the latter that the relations with our master sprang up to which we owe a small group of his very finest works, including the so-called *Venus of Urbino* of the Tribuna, the *Girl in a Fur Cloak* of the Vienna Gallery, and the companion portraits of Francesco Maria and Eleonora which are now in the Venetian Gallery at the Uffizi. The fiery leader of armies had, it should be remembered, been brought up by Guidobaldo of Montefeltro, one of the most amiable and enlightened princes of his time, and, moreover, his consort Eleonora was the daughter of Isabella d'Este Gonzaga, than whom the Renaissance knew no more enthusiastic or more discriminating patron of art.

A curious problem meets us at the outset. We may assume with some degree of certainty that the portraits of the duke and duchess belong to the year 1537. Stylistic characteristics point to the conclusion that the great *Venus* of the Tribuna, the so-called *Bella di Tiziano*, and the *Girl in the Fur Cloak* – to take only undoubted originals – belong to much the same stage of Titian's practice as the companion portraits at the Uffizi. Eleonora Gonzaga, a princess of the highest culture, the daughter of an admirable mother, the friend of Pietro Bembo, Sadolet, and Baldassarre Castiglione, was at this time a matron of some twenty years' standing; at the date when her avowed portrait was painted she must have been at the very least forty. By what magic did Titian manage to suggest her type and physiognomy in the famous pictures just now mentioned, and yet to plunge the duchess into a kind of *Fontaine de Jouvence*, realising in the divine freshness of youth and beauty beings who nevertheless appear to have with her some kind of mystic and unsolved connection? If this was what he really intended – and the results attained may lead us without temerity to assume as much – no subtler or more exquisite form of flattery could be conceived. It is curious to note that at the same time he signally failed with the portrait of her mother, Isabella d'Este, painted in 1534, but showing the Marchioness of Mantua as a young woman of some twenty-five years, though she was then sixty. Here youth and a semblance of beauty are called up by the magic of the artist, but the personality, both physical and mental, is lost in the effort. But then in this last case Titian was working from an early portrait, and without the living original to refer to.

But, before approaching the discussion of the *Venus of Urbino*, it is necessary to say a word about another *Venus* which must have been painted some years before this time, revealing, as it does, a completely different and, it must be owned, a higher ideal. This is the terribly ruined, yet still beautiful, *Venus Anadyomene*, or *Venus of the Shell*, of the Bridgewater Gallery, painted perhaps at the instigation of some humanist, to realise a description of the world-famous painting of Apelles. It is not at present possible to place this picture with anything approaching to chronological exactitude. It must have been painted some years after the *Bacchus and Ariadne* of the National Gallery, some years before the *Venus* of the Tribuna, and that is about as near as surmise can get. The type of the goddess in the Ellesmere picture recalls somewhat the *Ariadne* in our masterpiece at the National Gallery, but also, albeit in a less material form, the *Magdalens* of a later time. Titian's conception of perfect womanhood is here midway between his earlier Giorgionesque ideal and the frankly sensuous yet grand luxuriance of his maturity and old age. He never, even in the days of youth and Giorgionesque enchantment, penetrated so far below the surface as did his master and friend Barbarelli. He could not equal him in giving, with the undisguised physical allurement which belongs to the true woman, as distinguished from the ideal conception compounded of womanhood's finest attributes, that sovereignty of amorous yet of spiritual charm which is its complement and its corrective.[*16]

Still with Titian, too, in the earlier years, woman, as presented in the perfection of mature youth, had, accompanying and elevating her bodily loveliness, a measure of that higher and nobler feminine attractiveness which would enable her to meet man on equal terms, nay, actively to exercise a dominating influence of fascination. In illustration of this assertion it is only necessary to refer to the draped and the undraped figure in the *Medea and Venus (Sacred and Profane Love)* of the Borghese Gallery, to the *Herodias* of the Doria Gallery, to the *Flora* of the Uffizi. Here, even when the beautiful Venetian courtesan is represented or suggested, what the master gives is less the mere votary than the priestess of love. Of this power of domination, this feminine royalty, the *Venus Anadyomene* still retains a measure, but the *Venus of Urbino* and the splendid succession of Venuses and Danaës, goddesses, nymphs, and heroines belonging to the period of the fullest maturity, show woman in the phase in which, renouncing her power to enslave, she is herself reduced to slavery.

These glowing presentments of physical attractiveness embody a lower ideal – that of woman as the plaything of man, his precious possession, his delight in the lower sense. And yet Titian expresses this by no means exalted conception with a grand candour, an absence of *arrière-pensée* such as almost purges it of offence. It is Giovanni Morelli who, in tracing the gradual descent from his recovered treasure, the *Venus* of Giorgione in the Dresden Gallery,[*17] through the various Venuses of Titian down to those of the latest manner, so finely expresses the essential difference between Giorgione's divinity and her sister in the Tribuna. The former sleeping, and protected only by her sovereign loveliness, is safer from offence than the waking goddess – or shall we not rather say woman? – who in Titian's canvas passively waits in her rich Venetian bower, tended by her handmaidens. It is again Morelli[*18] who points out that, as compared with Correggio, even Giorgione – to say nothing of Titian – is when he renders the beauty of woman or goddess a realist. And this is true in a sense, yet not altogether. Correggio's *Danaë*, his *Io*, his *Leda*, his *Venus*, are in their exquisite grace of form and movement farther removed from the mere fleshly beauty of the undraped model than are the goddesses and women of Giorgione. The passion and throb of humanity are replaced by a subtler and less easily explicable charm; beauty becomes a perfectly balanced and finely modulated harmony. Still the allurement is there, and it is more consciously and more provocatively exercised than with Giorgione, though the fascination of Correggio's divinities asserts itself less directly, less candidly. Showing through the frankly human loveliness of Giorgione's women there is after all a higher spirituality, a deeper intimation of that true, that clear-burning passion, enveloping body and soul, which transcends all exterior grace and harmony, however exquisite it may be in refinement of voluptuousness.[*19]

It is not, indeed, by any means certain that we are justified in seriously criticising as a *Venus* the great picture of the Tribuna. Titian himself has given no indication that the beautiful Venetian woman who lies undraped after the bath, while in a sumptuous chamber, furnished according to the mode of the time, her handmaidens are seeking for the robes with which she will adorn herself, is intended to present the love-goddess, or even a beauty masquerading with her attributes. Vasari, who saw it in the picture-closet of the Duke of Urbino, describes it, no doubt, as "une Venere giovanetta a giacere, con fieri e certi panni sottili attorno." It is manifestly borrowed, too – as is now universally acknowledged – from Giorgione's *Venus* in the Dresden Gallery, with the significant alteration, however, that Titian's fair one voluptuously dreams awake, while Giorgione's goddess more divinely reposes, and sleeping dreams loftier dreams. The motive is in the borrowing robbed of much of its dignity and beauty, and individualised in a fashion which, were any other master than Titian in question, would have brought it to the verge of triviality. Still as an example of his unrivalled mastery in rendering the glow and semi-transparency of flesh, enhanced by the contrast with white linen – itself slightly golden in tinge; in suggesting the appropriate atmospheric environment; in giving the full splendour of Venetian colour, duly subordinated nevertheless to the main motive, which is the glorification of a beautiful human body as it is; in all these respects the picture is of superlative excellence, a representative example of the master and of Venetian art, a piece which it would not be easy to match even among his own works.

More and more, as the supreme artist matures, do we find him disdaining the showier and more evident forms of virtuosity. His colour is more and more marked in its luminous beauty by reticence and concentration, by the search after such a main colour-chord as shall not only be beautiful and satisfying in itself, but expressive of the motive which is at the root of the picture. Play of light over the surfaces and round the contours of the human form; the breaking-up and modulation of masses of colour by that play of light; strength, and beauty of general tone – these are now Titian's main preoccupations. To this point his perfected technical art has legitimately developed itself from the Giorgionesque ideal of colour and tone-harmony, which was essentially the same in principle, though necessarily in a less advanced stage, and more diversified by exceptions. Our master became, as time went on, less and less interested in the mere dexterous juxtaposition of brilliantly harmonising and brilliantly contrasting tints, in piquancy, gaiety, and sparkle of colour, to be achieved for its own sake. Indeed this phase of Venetian sixteenth-century colour belongs rather to those artists who issued from Verona – to the Bonifazi, and to Paolo Veronese – who in this respect, as generally in artistic temperament, proved themselves the natural successors of Domenico and Francesco Morone, of Girolamo dai Libri, of Cavazzola.

Yet when Titian takes colour itself as his chief motive, he can vie with the most sumptuous of them in splendour, and eclipse them all by the sureness of his taste. A good example of this is the celebrated *Bella di Tiziano* of the Pitti Gallery, another work which, like the *Venus of Urbino*, recalls the features without giving the precise personality of Eleonora Gonzaga. The beautiful but somewhat expressionless head with its crowning glory of bright hair, a waving mass of Venetian gold, has been so much injured by rubbing down and restoration that we regret what has been lost even more than we enjoy what is left. But the surfaces of the fair and exquisitely modelled neck and bosom have been less cruelly treated; the superb costume retains much of its pristine splendour. With its combination of brownish-purple velvet, peacock-blue brocade, and white lawn, its delicate trimmings of gold, and its further adornment with small knots, having in them, now at any rate, but an effaced note of red, the gown of *La Bella* has remained the type of what is most beautiful in Venetian costume as it was in the earlier half of the sixteenth century. In richness and ingenious elaboration, chastened by taste, it far transcends the over-splendid and ponderous dresses in which later on the patrician dames portrayed by Veronese and his school loved to array themselves. A bright note of red in the upper jewel of one earring, now, no doubt, cruder than was originally intended, gives a fillip to the whole, after a fashion peculiar to Titian.

The *Girl in the Fur Cloak*, No 197 in the Imperial Gallery at Vienna, shows once more in a youthful and blooming woman the features of Eleonora. The model is nude under a mantle of black satin lined with fur, which leaves uncovered the right breast and both arms. The picture is undoubtedly Titian's own, and fine in quality, but it reveals less than his usual graciousness and charm. It is probably identical with the canvas described in the often-quoted catalogue of Charles I.'s pictures as "A naked woman putting on her smock, which the king changed with the Duchess of Buckingham for one of His Majesty's Mantua pieces." It may well have suggested to Rubens, who must have seen it among the King's possessions on the occasion of his visit to London, his superb, yet singularly unrefined, *Hélène Fourment in a Fur*

Mantle, now also in the Vienna Gallery.

The great portraits of the Duke and Duchess of Urbino in the Uffizi belong, as has already been noted, to 1537. Francesco Maria, here represented in the penultimate year of his stormy life, assumes deliberately the truculent warrior, and has beyond reasonable doubt made his own pose in a portrait destined to show the leader of armies, and not the amorous spouse or the patron of art and artists. Praise enthusiastic, but not excessive, has ever been and ever will be lavished on the breadth and splendid decision of the painting; on the magnificent rendering of the suit of plain but finely fashioned steel armour, with its wonderful reflections; on the energy of the virile countenance, and the appropriate concentration and simplicity of the whole. The superb head has, it must be confessed, more grandeur and energy than true individuality or life. The companion picture represents Eleonora Gonzaga seated near an open window, wearing a sombre but magnificent costume, and, completing it, one of those turbans with which the patrician ladies of North Italy, other than those of Venice, habitually crowned their locks. It has suffered in loss of freshness and touch more than its companion. Fine and accurate as the portrait is, much as it surpasses its pendant in subtle truth of characterisation, it has in the opinion of the writer been somewhat overpraised. For once, Titian approaches very nearly to the northern ideal in portraiture, underlining the truth with singular accuracy, yet with some sacrifice of graciousness and charm. The daughter of the learned and brilliant Isabella looks here as if, in the decline of her beauty, she had become something of a *précieuse* and a prude, though it would be imprudent to assert that she was either the one or the other. Perhaps the most attractive feature of the whole composition is the beautiful landscape so characteristically stretching away into the far blue distance, suggested rather than revealed through the open window. This is such a picture as might have inspired the Netherlander Antonio Moro, just because it is Italian art of the Cinquecento with a difference, that is, with a certain admixture of northern downrightness and literalness of statement.

About this same time Titian received from the brother of this princess, his patron and admirer Federigo Gonzaga, the commission for the famous series of the *Twelve Cæsars*, now only known to the world by stray copies here and there, and by the grotesquely exaggerated engravings of Ægidius Sadeler. Giulio Romano having in 1536[*20] completed the Sala di Troja in the Castello of Mantua, and made considerable progress with the apartments round about it, Federigo Gonzaga conceived the idea of devoting one whole room to the painted effigies of the *Twelve Cæsars* to be undertaken by Titian. The exact date when the *Cæsars* were delivered is not known, but it may legitimately be inferred that this was in the course of 1537 or the earlier half of 1538. Our master's pictures were, according to Vasari, placed in an *anticamera* of the Mantuan Palace, below them being hung twelve *storie a olio* – histories in oils – by Giulio Romano.[*21] The *Cæsars* were all half-lengths, eleven out of the twelve being done by the Venetian master and the twelfth by Giulio Romano himself.[*22] Brought to England with the rest of the Mantua pieces purchased by Daniel Nys for Charles I., they suffered injury, and Van Dyck is said to have repainted the *Vitellius*, which was one of several canvases irretrievably ruined by the quicksilver of the frames during the transit from Italy.[*23] On the disposal of the royal collection after Charles Stuart's execution the *Twelve Cæsars* were sold by the State – not presented, as is usually asserted – to the Spanish Ambassador Cardenas, who gave £1200 for them. On their arrival in Spain with the other treasures secured on behalf of Philip IV., they were placed in the Alcazar of Madrid, where in one of the numerous fires which successively devastated the royal palace they must have perished, since no trace of them is to be found after the end of the seventeenth century. The popularity of Titian's decorative canvases is proved by the fact that Bernardino Campi of Cremona made five successive sets of copies from them – for Charles V., d'Avalos, the Duke of Alva, Rangone, and another Spanish grandee. Agostino

Caracci subsequently copied them for the palace of Parma, and traces of yet other copies exist. Numerous versions are shown in private collections, both in England and abroad, purporting to be from the hand of Titian, but of these none – at any rate none of those seen by the writer – are originals or even Venetian copies. Among the best are the examples in the collection of Earl Brownlow and at the royal palace of Munich respectively, and these may possibly be from the hand of Campi. Although we are expressly told in Dolce's *Dialogo* that Titian "painted the *Twelve Cæsars*, taking them in part from medals, in part from antique marbles," it is perfectly clear that of the exact copying of antiques – such as is to be noted, for instance, in those marble medallions by Donatello which adorn the courtyard of the Medici Palace at Florence – there can have been no question. The attitudes of the *Cæsars*, as shown in the engravings and the extant copies, exclude any such supposition. Those who have judged them from those copies and the hideous grotesques of Sadeler have wondered at the popularity of the originals, somewhat hastily deeming Titian to have been here inferior to himself. Strange to say, a better idea of what he intended, and what he may have realised in the originals, is to be obtained from a series of small copies now in the Provincial Museum of Hanover, than from anything else that has survived.[*24] The little pictures in question, being on copper, cannot well be anterior to the first part of the seventeenth century, and they are not in themselves wonders. All the same they have a unique interest as proving that, while adopting the pompous attitudes and the purely decorative standpoint which the position of the pictures in the Castello may have rendered obligatory, Titian managed to make of his Emperors creatures of flesh and blood; the splendid Venetian warrior and patrician appearing in all the glory of manhood behind the conventional dignity, the self-consciousness of the Roman type and attitude.

These last years had been to Titian as fruitful in material gain as in honour. He had, as has been seen, established permanent and intimate relations not only with the art-loving rulers of the

North Italian principalities, but now with Charles V. himself, mightiest of European sovereigns, and, as a natural consequence, with the all-powerful captains and grandees of the Hispano-Austrian court. Meanwhile a serious danger to his supremacy had arisen. At home in Venice his unique position was threatened by Pordenone, that masterly and wonderfully facile *frescante* and painter of monumental decorations, who had on more than one occasion in the past been found in competition with him.

The Friulan, after many wanderings and much labour in North Italy, had settled in Venice in 1535, and there acquired an immense reputation by the grandeur and consummate ease with which he had carried out great mural decorations, such as the façade of Martin d'Anna's house on the Grand Canal, comprising in its scheme of decoration a Curtius on horse-back and a flying Mercury which according to Vasari became the talk of the town.[*25] Here, at any rate, was a field in which even Titian himself, seeing that he had only at long intervals practised in fresco painting, could not hope to rival Pordenone. The Friulan, indeed, in this his special branch, stood entirely alone among the painters of North Italy.

The Council of Ten in June 1537 issued a decree recording that Titian had since 1516 been in possession of his *senseria*, or broker's patent, and its accompanying salary, on condition that he should paint "the canvas of the land fight on the side of the Hall of the Great Council looking out on the Grand Canal," but that he had drawn his salary without performing his promise. He was therefore called upon to refund all that he had received for the time during which he had done no work. This sharp reminder operated as it was intended to do. We see from Aretino's correspondence that in November 1537 Titian was busily engaged on the great canvas for the Doges' Palace. This tardy recognition of an old obligation did not prevent the Council from issuing an order in November 1538 directing Pordenone to paint a picture for the Sala del Gran Consiglio, to occupy the space next to that reserved for Titian's long-delayed battle-piece.

That this can never have been executed is clear, since Pordenone, on receipt of an urgent summons from Ercole II., Duke of Ferrara, departed from Venice in the month of December of the same year, and falling sick at Ferrara, died so suddenly as to give rise to the suspicion of foul play, which too easily sprang up in those days when ambition or private vengeance found ready to hand weapons so many and so convenient. Crowe and Cavalcaselle give good grounds for the assumption that, in order to save appearances, Titian was supposed – replacing and covering the battle-piece which already existed in the Great Hall – to be presenting the Battle of Spoleto in Umbria, whereas it was clear to all Venetians, from the costumes, the banners, and the landscape, that he meant to depict the Battle of Cadore fought in 1508. The latter was a Venetian victory and an Imperial defeat, the former a Papal defeat and an Imperial victory. The all-devouring fire of 1577 annihilated the *Battle of Cadore* with too many other works of capital importance in the history both of the primitive and the mature Venetian schools. We have nothing now to show what it may have been, save the print of Fontana, and the oil painting in the Venetian Gallery of the Uffizi, reproducing on a reduced scale part only of the big canvas. This last is of Venetian origin, and more or less contemporary, but it need hardly be pointed out that it is a copy from, not a sketch for, the picture.

To us who know the vast battle-piece only in the feeble echo of the print and the picture just now mentioned, it is a little difficult to account for the enthusiasm that it excited, and the prominent place accorded to it among the most famous of the Cadorine's works. Though the whole has abundant movement and passion, and the *mise-en-scène* is undoubtedly imposing, the combat is not raised above reality into the region of the higher and more representative truth by any element of tragic vastness and significance. Even though the Imperialists are armed more or less in the antique Roman fashion, to distinguish them from the Venetians, who appear in the accoutrements of their own day, it is still that minor and local combat the *Battle of Cadore* that we have before us, and not, above and beyond this battle, War, as some masters of the century, gifted with a higher power of evocation, might have shown it. Even as the fragment of Leonardo da Vinci's *Battle of Anghiari* survives in the free translation of Rubens's well-known drawing in the Louvre, we see how he has made out of the unimportant cavalry combat, yet without conventionality or undue transposition, a representation unequalled in art of the frenzy generated in man and beast by the clash of arms and the scent of blood. And Rubens, too, how incomparably in the *Battle of the Amazons* of the Pinakothek at Munich, he evokes the terrors, not only of one mortal encounter, but of War – the hideous din, the horror of man let loose and become beast once more, the pitiless yell of the victors, the despairing cry of the vanquished, the irremediable overthrow! It would, however, be foolhardy in those who can only guess at what the picture may have been to arrogate to themselves the right of sitting in judgment on Vasari and those contemporaries who, actually seeing, enthusiastically admired it. What excited their delight must surely have been Titian's magic power of brush as displayed in individual figures and episodes, such as that famous one of the knight armed by his page in the immediate foreground.

Into this period of our master's career there fit very well the two portraits in which he appears, painted by himself, on the confines of old age, vigorous and ardent still, fully conscious, moreover, though without affectation, of pre-eminent genius and supreme artistic rank. The portraits referred to are those very similar ones, both of them undoubtedly originals, which are respectively in the Berlin Gallery and the Painters' Gallery of the Uffizi. It is strange that there should exist no certain likeness of the master of Cadore done in youth or earlier manhood, if there be excepted the injured and more than doubtful production in the Imperial Gallery of Vienna, which has pretty generally been supposed to be an original auto-portrait belonging to this period. In the Uffizi and Berlin pictures Titian looks about sixty years old, but may be a little more or a little less. The latter is a half-length, showing him seated and gazing obliquely out of the picture with a majestic air, but also with something of combativeness and disquietude, an element, this last, which is traceable even in some of the earlier portraits, but not in the mythological *poesie* or any sacred work. More and more as we advance through the final period of old age do we find this element of disquietude and misgiving asserting itself in male portraiture, as, for instance, in the *Maltese Knight* of the Prado, the *Dominican Monk* of the Borghese, the *Portrait of a Man with a Palm Branch* of the Dresden Gallery. The atmosphere of sadness and foreboding enveloping man is traceable back to Giorgione; but with him it comes from the plenitude of inner life, from the gaze turned inwards upon the mystery of the human individuality rather than outwards upon the inevitable tragedies of the exterior life common to all. This same atmosphere of passionate contemplativeness enwraps, indeed, all that Giorgione did, and is the cause that he sees the world and himself lyrically, not dramatically; the flame of aspiration burning steadily at the heart's core and leaving the surface not indeed unruffled, but outwardly calm in its glow. Titian's is the more dramatic temperament in outward things, but also the more superficial. It must be remembered, too, that arriving rapidly at the maturity of his art, and painting all through the period of the full Renaissance, he was able with far less hindrance from technical limitations to express his conceptions to the full. His portraiture, however, especially his male portraiture, was and remained in its essence a splendid and full-blown development of the Giorgionesque ideal. It was grander, more accomplished, and for obvious reasons more satisfying, yet far less penetrating, less expressive of the inner fibre, whether of the painter or of his subject.

But to return to the portrait of Berlin. It is in parts unfinished, and therefore the more interesting as revealing something of the methods employed by the master in this period of absolute mastery, when his palette was as sober in its strength as it was rich and harmonious; when, as ever, execution was a way to an end, and therefore not to be vain-gloriously displayed merely for its own sake. The picture came, with very many other master-pieces of the Italian and Netherlandish schools, from the Solly collection, which formed the nucleus of the Berlin Gallery. The Uffizi portrait emerges noble still, in its semi-ruined state, from a haze of restoration and injury, which has not succeeded in destroying the exceptional fineness and sensitiveness of the modelling. Although the pose and treatment of the head are practically identical with that in the Berlin picture, the conception seems a less dramatic one. It includes, unless the writer has misread it, an element of greater mansuetude and a less perturbed reflectiveness.

The double portrait in the collection of Her Majesty the Queen at Windsor Castle, styled *Titian and Franceschini*[*26] has no pretensions whatever to be even discussed as a Titian. The figure of the Venetian senator designated as Franceschini is the better performance of the two; the lifeless head of Titian, which looks very like an afterthought, has been copied, without reference to the relation of the two figures the one to the other, from the Uffizi picture, or some portrait identical with it in character. A far finer likeness of Titian than any of these is the much later one, now in the Prado Gallery; but this it will be best to deal with in its proper chronological order.

We come now to one of the most popular of all Titian's great canvases based on a sacred subject, the *Presentation in the Temple* in the Accademia delle Belle Arti at Venice. This, as Vasari expressly states, was painted for the Scuola di S. Maria della Carità, that is, for the confraternity which owned the very building where now the Accademia displays its treasures. It is the magnificent scenic rendering of a subject lending itself easily to exterior pomp and display, not so easily to a more mystic and less obvious mode of conception. At the root of Titian's design lies in all probability the very similar picture on a comparatively small scale by Cima da Conegliano, now No. 63 in the Dresden Gallery, and this last may well have been inspired by Carpaccio's *Presentation of the Virgin,* now in the Brera at Milan.[*27] The imposing canvases belonging to this particular period of Titian's activity, and this one in particular, with its splendid architectural framing, its wealth of life and movement, its richness and variety in type and costume, its fair prospect of Venetian landscape in the distance, must have largely contributed to form the transcendent decorative talent of Paolo Veronese. Only in the exquisitely fresh and beautiful figure of the childlike Virgin, who ascends the mighty flight of stone steps, clad all in shimmering blue, her head crowned with a halo of yellow light, does the artist prove that he has penetrated to the innermost significance of his subject. Here, at any rate, he touches the heart as well as feasts the eye. The thoughts of all who are familiar with Venetian art will involuntarily turn to Tintoretto's rendering of the same moving, yet in its symbolical character not naturally ultra-dramatic, scene. The younger master lends to it a significance so vast that he may be said to go as far beyond and above the requirements of the theme as Titian, with all his legitimate splendour and serene dignity, remains below it. With Tintoretto as interpreter we are made to see the beautiful episode as an event of the most tremendous import – one that must shake the earth to its centre. The reason of the onlooker may rebel against this portentous version, yet he is dominated all the same, is overwhelmed with something of the indefinable awe that has seized upon the bystanders who are witnesses of the scene.

But now to discuss a very curious point in connection with the actual state of Titian's important canvas. It has been very generally assumed – and Crowe and Cavalcaselle have set their seal on the assumption – that Titian painted his picture for a special place in the Albergo (now Accademia), and that this place is now architecturally as it was in Titian's time. Let them speak for themselves.

"In this room (in the Albergo), which is contiguous to the modern hall

in which Titian's *Assunta* is displayed, there were two doors for
which allowance was made in Titian's canvas; twenty-five feet – the
length of the wall – is now the length of the picture. When this vast
canvas was removed from its place, the gaps of the doors were filled
in with new linen, and painted up to the tone of the original...."

That the pieces of canvas to which reference is here made
were new, and not Titian's original work from the brush, was of
course well known to those who saw the work as it used to hang
in the Accademia. Crowe and Cavalcaselle give indeed the name
of a painter of this century who is responsible for them. Within
the last three years the new and enterprising director of the
Venice Academy, as part of a comprehensive scheme of
rearrangement of the whole collection, caused these pieces of new
canvas to be removed and then proceeded to replace the picture
in the room for which it is believed to have been executed, fitting
it into the space above the two doors just referred to. Many people
have declared themselves delighted with the alteration, looking
upon it as a tardy act of justice done to Titian, whose work, it is
assumed, is now again seen just as he designed it for the Albergo.
The writer must own that he has, from an examination of the
canvas where it is now placed, or replaced, derived an absolutely
contrary impression. First, is it conceivable that Titian in the
heyday of his glory should have been asked to paint such a
picture – not a mere mural decoration – for such a place? There is
no instance of anything of the kind having been done with the
canvases painted by Gentile Bellini, Carpaccio, Mansueti, and
others for the various *Scuole* of Venice. There is no instance of a
great decorative canvas by a sixteenth century master of the first
rank,[*28] other than a ceiling decoration, being degraded in the
first instance to such a use. And then Vasari, who saw the picture
in Venice, and correctly characterises it, would surely have
noticed such an extraordinary peculiarity as the abnormal shape
necessitated by the two doors. It is incredible that Titian, if so
unpalatable a task had indeed been originally imposed upon
him, should not have designed his canvas otherwise. The hole for

the right door coming in the midst of the monumental steps is just possible, though not very probable. Not so that for the left door, which, according to the present arrangement, cuts the very vitals out of one of the main groups in the foreground. Is it not to insult one of the greatest masters of all time thus to assume that he would have designed what we now see? It is much more likely that Titian executed his *Presentation* in the first place in the normal shape, and that vandals of a later time, deciding to pierce the room in the Scuola in which the picture is now once more placed with one, or probably two, additional doors, partially sacrificed it to the structural requirements of the moment. Monstrous as such barbarism may appear, we have already seen, and shall again see later on, that it was by no means uncommon in those great ages of painting, the sixteenth and seventeenth centuries.

When the untimely death of Pordenone, at the close of 1538, had extinguished the hopes of the Council that the grandiose facility of this master of monumental decoration might be made available for the purposes of the State, Titian having, as has been seen, made good his gravest default, was reinstated in his lucrative and by no means onerous office. He regained the *senseria* by decree of August 28, 1539. The potent d'Avalos, Marqués del Vasto, had in 1539 conferred upon Titian's eldest son Pomponio, the scapegrace and spendthrift that was to be, a canonry. Both to father and son the gift was in the future to be productive of more evil than good. At or about the same time he had commissioned of Titian a picture of himself haranguing his soldiers in the pompous Roman fashion; this was not, however, completed until 1541. Exhibited by d'Avalos to admiring crowds at Milan, it made a sensation for which there is absolutely nothing in the picture, as we now see it in the gallery of the Prado, to account; but then it would appear that it was irreparably injured in a fire which devastated the Alcazar of Madrid in 1621, and was afterwards extensively repainted. The Marquis and his son Francesco, both of them full-length figures, are placed on a low plinth, to the left, and from this point of vantage the Spanish leader addresses a company of foot-soldiers who with fine effect raise their halberds high into the air.[*29] Among these last tradition places a portrait of Aretino, which is not now to be recognised with any certainty. Were the pedigree of the canvas a less well-authenticated one, one might be tempted to deny Titian's authorship altogether, so extraordinary are, apart from other considerations, the disproportions in the figure of the youth Francesco. Restoration must in this instance have amounted to entire repainting. Del Vasto appears more robust, more martial, and slightly younger than the armed leader in the *Allegory* of the Louvre. If this last picture is to be accepted as a semi-idealised presentment of the Spanish captain, it must, as has already been pointed out, have been painted nearer to the time of his death, which took place in 1546. The often-cited biographers of our master are clearly in error in their conclusion that the painting described in the collection of Charles I. as "done by Titian, the picture of the Marquis Guasto, containing five half-figures so big as the life, which the king bought out of an Almonedo," is identical with the large sketch made by Titian as a preparation for the *Allocution* of Madrid. This description, on the contrary, applies perfectly to the *Allegory* of the Louvre, which was, as we know, included in the collection of Charles, and subsequently found its way into that of Louis Quatorze.

It was in 1542 that Vasari, summoned to Venice at the suggestion of Aretino, paid his first visit to the city of the Lagoons in order to paint the scenery and *apparato* in connection with a carnival performance, which included the representation of his fellow-townsman's *Talanta*.[*30] It was on this occasion, no doubt, that Sansovino, in agreement with Titian, obtained for the Florentine the commission to paint the ceilings of Santo Spirito in Isola – a commission which was afterwards, as a consequence of his departure, undertaken and performed by Titian himself, with whose grandiose canvases we shall have to deal a little later on. In weighing the value of Vasari's testimony with reference to the works of Vecellio and other Venetian painters more or less of his own time, it should be borne in mind that he paid two successive visits to Venice, enjoying there the company of the great painter and the most eminent artists of the day, and that on the occasion of Titian's memorable visit to Rome he was his close friend, cicerone, and companion. Allowing for the Aretine biographer's well-known inaccuracies in matters of detail and for his royal disregard of chronological order – faults for which it is manifestly absurd to blame him over-severely – it would be unwise lightly to disregard or overrule his testimony with regard to matters which he may have learned from the lips of Titian himself and his immediate entourage.

To the year 1542 belongs, as the authentic signature and date on the picture affirm, that celebrated portrait, *The Daughter of Roberto Strozzi*, once in the splendid palace of the family at Florence, but now, with some other priceless treasures having the same origin, in the Berlin Museum. Technically, the picture is one of the most brilliant, one of the most subtly exquisite, among the works of the great Cadorine's maturity. It well serves to show what Titian's ideal of colour was at this time. The canvas is all silvery gleam, all splendour and sober strength of colour – yet not of colours. These in all their plentitude and richness, as in the crimson drapery and the distant landscape, are duly subordinated to the main effect; they but set off discreetly the figure of the child, dressed all in white satin with hair of reddish gold, and contribute without fanfare to the fine and harmonious balance of the whole. Here, as elsewhere, more particularly in the work of Titian's maturity, one does not in the first place pause to pick out this or the other tint, this or the other combination of colours as particularly exquisite; and that is what one is so easily led to do in the contemplation of the Bonifazi and of Paolo Veronese.

As the portrait of a child, though in conception it reveals a marked progress towards the *intimité* of later times, the Berlin picture lacks something of charm and that quality which, for want of a better word, must be called loveableness. Or is it perhaps that the eighteenth and nineteenth centuries have spoilt us in this respect? For it is only in these latter days that to the child, in deliberate and avowed portraiture, is allowed that freakishness, that natural *espièglerie* and freedom from artificial control which has its climax in the unapproached portraits of Sir Joshua Reynolds. This is the more curious when it is remembered how tenderly, with what observant and sympathetic truth the relation of child to mother, of child to child, was noted in the innumerable "Madonnas" and "Holy Families" of the fifteenth and sixteenth centuries; how both the Italians, and following them the Netherlanders, relieved the severity of their sacred works by the delightful roguishness, the romping impudence of their little angels, their *putti*.

It has already been recorded that Titian, taking up the commission abandoned by Vasari, undertook a great scheme of pictorial decoration for the Brothers of Santo Spirito in Isola. All that he carried out for that church has now found its way into that of the Salute. The three ceiling pictures, *The Sacrifice of Isaac, Cain and Abel,* and *David victorious over Goliath,* are in the great sacristy of the church; the *Four Evangelists* and *Four Doctors* are in the ceiling of the choir behind the altar; the altar-piece, *The Descent of the Holy Spirit,* is in one of the chapels which completely girdle the circular church itself. The ceiling pictures, depicting three of the most dramatic moments in sacred history, have received the most enthusiastic praise from the master's successive biographers. They were indeed at the time of their inception a new thing in Venetian art. Nothing so daring as these foreshortenings, as these scenes of dramatic violence, of physical force triumphant, had been seen in Venice. The turbulent spirit was an exaggeration of that revealed by Titian in the *St. Peter Martyr;* the problem of the foreshortening for the purposes of ceiling decoration was superadded. It must be remembered, too, that even in Rome, the headquarters of the grand style, nothing precisely of the same kind could be said to exist. Raphael and his pupils either disdained, or it may be feared to approach, the problem. Neither in the ceiling decorations of the Farnesina nor in the Stanze is there any attempt on a large scale to *faire plafonner* the figures, that is, to paint them so that they might appear as they would actually be seen from below. Michelangelo himself, in the stupendous decoration of the ceiling to the Sixtine Chapel, had elected to treat the subjects of the flat surface which constitutes the centre and climax of the whole, as a series of pictures designed under ordinary conditions. It can hardly be doubted that Titian, in attempting these *tours de force*, though not necessarily or even probably in any other way, was inspired by Correggio. It would not be easy, indeed, to exaggerate the Venetian master's achievement from this point of view, even though in two at least of the groups – the *Cain and Abel* and the *David and Goliath* – the modern professor might be justified in criticising with consider-able severity his draughtsmanship and many salient points in his design. The effect produced is tremendous of its kind. The power suggested is, however, brutal, unreasoning, not nobly domin-ating force; and this not alone in the *Cain and Abel*, where such an impression is rightly conveyed, but also in the other pieces. It is as if Titian, in striving to go beyond anything that had hitherto been done of the same kind, had also gone beyond his own artistic convictions, and thus, while compassing a remarkable pictorial achievement, lost his true balance. Tintoretto, creating his own atmosphere, as far outside and above mere physical realities as that of Michelangelo himself, might have succeeded in mitigating this impression, which is, on the whole, a painful one. Take for instance the *Martyrdom of St. Christopher* of the younger painter – not a ceiling picture by the way – in the apse of S. Maria del Orto. Here, too, is depicted, with sweeping and altogether irresistible power, an act of hideous violence. And yet it is not this element of the subject which makes upon the spectator the most profound effect, but the impression of saintly submission, of voluntary self-sacrifice, which is the dominant note of the whole.

It may be convenient to mention here *The Descent of the Holy Spirit*, although in its definitive form, as we see it in its place in the Church of the Salute, it appears markedly more advanced in style than the works of the period at which we have now arrived, giving, both in manner and feeling, a distinct suggestion of the methods and standpoint which mark the later phase of old age. Vasari tells us that the picture, originally painted in 1541, was seriously damaged and subsequently repainted; Crowe and Cavalcaselle state that the work now seen at the Salute was painted to replace an altar-piece which the Brothers of Santo Spirito had declined to accept. Even as the picture now appears, somewhat faded, and moreover seen at a disadvantage amid its cold surroundings of polished white marble, it is a composition of wonderful, of almost febrile animation, and a painting saturated with light, pierced through everywhere with its rays. The effect produced is absolutely that which the mystical subject requires.[*31] Abandoning the passionless serenity which has been the rule in sacred subjects of the middle time, Titian shows himself more stimulated, more moved by his subject.

It was in the spring of 1543 that the master first came into personal contact with Pope Paul III. and the Farnese family. The meeting took place at Ferrara, and our painter then accompanied the papal court to Busseto, and subsequently proceeded to Bologna. Aretino's correspondence proves that Titian must at that time have painted the Pope, and that he must also have refused the sovereign pontiff's offer of the *Piombo*, which was then still, as it had been for years past, in the possession of Sebastiano Luciani. That Titian, with all his eagerness for wealth and position, could not find it in his heart to displace his fellow-countryman, a friend no doubt of the early time, may legitimately excite admiration and sympathy now, as according to Aretino it actually did at the time. The portraits of the Farnese family included that of the Pope, repeated subsequently for Cardinal Santafiore, that of Pier Luigi, then that of Paul III. and this monstrous yet well-loved son together,[*32] and a likeness of Cardinal Alessandro Farnese. Upon the three-quarter length portrait of Paul III. in the Naples Museum, Crowe and Cavalcaselle have lavished their most enthusiastic praise, placing it, indeed, among his masterpieces.

All the same – interesting as the picture undoubtedly is, remarkable in finish, and of undoubtedly Titianesque origin – the writer finds it difficult, nay impossible, to accept this *Paul III.* as a work from the hand of Titian himself. Careful to excess, and for such an original too much wanting in brilliancy and vitality, it is the best of many repetitions and variations; of this particular type the original is not at present forthcoming. Very different is the "Paul III." of the Hermitage, which even in a reproduction loudly proclaims its originality.[*33] This is by no means identical in design with the Naples picture, but appears much less studied, much more directly taken from the life. The astute Farnese Pope has here the same simiesque type, the same furtive distrustful look, as in the great unfinished group now to be described.[*34] This Titian, which doubtless passed into the Hermitage with the rest of the Barbarigo pictures, may have been the first foundation for the series of portraits of the Farnese Pope, and as such would naturally have been retained by the master for his own use. The portrait-group in the Naples Museum, showing, with Paul III., Cardinal Alessandro Farnese and Ottavio Farnese (afterwards Duke of Parma), is, apart from its extraordinary directness and swift technical mastery, of exceptional interest as being unfinished, and thus doubly instructive. The composition, lacking in its unusual momentariness the repose and dignity of Raphael's *Leo X. with Cardinals Giulio de' Medici and de' Rossi* at the Pitti, is not wholly happy. Especially is the action of Ottavio Farnese, as in reverence he bends down to reply to the supreme Pontiff, forced and unconvincing; but the unflattered portrait of the pontiff himself is of a bold and quite unconventional truth, and in movement much happier. The picture may possibly, by reason of this unconventional conception less than perfectly realised, have failed to please the sitters, and thus have been left in its present state.[*35]

Few of Titian's canvases of vast dimensions have enjoyed a higher degree of popularity than the large *Ecce Homo* to which the Viennese proudly point as one of the crowning ornaments of the great Imperial Gallery of their city. Completed in 1543[*36] for Giovanni d'Anna, a son of the Flemish merchant Martin van der Hanna, who had established himself in Venice, it was vainly coveted by Henri III. on the occasion of his memorable visit in 1574, but was in 1620 purchased for the splendid favourite, George Villiers, Duke of Buckingham, by the English envoy Sir Henry Wotton. From him the noblest and most accomplished of English collectors, Thomas, Earl of Arundel, sought to obtain the prize with the unparalleled offer of £7000, yet even thus failed. At the time of the great *débâcle*, in 1648, the guardians and advisers of his youthful son and successor were glad enough to get the splendid gallery over to the Low Countries, and to sell with the rest the *Ecce Homo*, which brought under these circumstances but a tenth part of what Lord Arundel would have given for it. Passing into the collection of the Archduke Leopold William, it was later on finally incorporated with that of the Imperial House of Austria. From the point of view of scenic and decorative magnificence combined with dramatic propriety, though not with any depth or intensity of dramatic passion, the work is undoubtedly imposing. Yet it suffers somewhat, even in this respect, from the fact that the figures are not more than small life-size. With passages of Titianesque splendour there are to be noted others, approaching to the acrid and inharmonious, which one would rather attribute to the master's assistants than to himself. So it is, too, with certain exaggerations of design characteristic rather of the period than the man – notably with the two figures to the left of the foreground. The Christ in His meekness is too little divine, too heavy and inert;[*37] the Pontius Pilate not inappropriately reproduces the features of the worldling and *viveur* Aretino. The mounted warrior to the extreme right, who has been supposed to represent Alfonso d'Este, shows the genial physiognomy made familiar by the Madrid picture so long deemed to be his portrait, but which, as has already been pointed out, represents much more probably his successor Ercole II. d'Este, whom we find again in that superb piece by the master, the so-called *Giorgio Cornaro* of Castle Howard. The *Ecce Homo* of Vienna is another of the works of which both the general *ordonnance* and the truly Venetian splendour must have profoundly influenced Paolo Veronese.

To this period belongs also the *Annunciation of the Virgin* now in the Cathedral of Verona – a rich, harmonious, and appropriate altar-piece, but not one of any special significance in the life-work of the painter.

Shall we not, pretty much in agreement with Vasari, place here, just before the long-delayed visit to Rome, the *Christ with the Pilgrims at Emmaus* of the Louvre? A strong reason for dating this, one of the noblest, one of the most deeply felt of all Titian's works, before rather than after the stay in the Eternal City, is that in its *naïveté*, in its realistic episodes, in its fulness of life, it is so entirely and delightfully Venetian. Here again the colour-harmony in its subdued richness and solemnity has a completeness such as induces the beholder to accept it in its unity rather than to analyse those infinite subtleties of juxtaposition and handling which, avoiding bravura, disdain to show themselves on the surface. The sublime beauty of the landscape, in which, as often elsewhere, the golden radiance of the setting sun is seen battling with masses of azure cloud, has not been exceeded by Titian himself. With all the daring yet perfectly unobtrusive and unconscious realism of certain details, the conception is one of the loftiest, one of the most penetrating in its very simplicity, of Venetian art at its apogee. The divine mansuetude, the human and brotherly sympathy of the Christ, have not been equalled since the early days of the *Cristo della Moneta*. Altogether the *Pilgrims at Emmaus* well marks that higher and more far-reaching conception of sacred art which reveals itself in the productions of Titian's old age, when we compare them with the untroubled serenity and the conventional assumptions of the middle time.[*38]

To the year 1545 belongs the supremely fine *Portrait of Aretino*, which is one of the glories of the Pitti Gallery. This was destined to propitiate the Grand Duke Cosimo of Tuscany, the son of his passionately attached friend of earlier days, Giovanni delle Bande Nere. Aretino, who had particular reasons for desiring to appear before the obdurate Cosimo in all the pomp and opulence of his later years, was obviously wounded that Titian, true to his genius, and to his method at this moment, should have made the keynote of his masterpiece a dignified simplicity. For once unfaithful to his brother Triumvir and friend, he attacks him in the accompanying letter to the Tuscan ruler with the withering sarcasm that "the satins, velvets, and brocades would perhaps have been better if Titian had received a few more scudi for working them out." If Aretino's pique had not caused the momentary clouding over of his artistic vision, he would have owned that the canvas now in the Pitti was one of the happiest achievements of Titian and one of the greatest things in portraiture. There is no flattery here of the "Divine Aretino," as with heroic impudence the notorious publicist styles himself. The sensual type is preserved, but rendered acceptable, and in a sense attractive, by a certain assurance and even dignity of bearing, such as success and a position impregnable of its unique and unenviable kind may well have lent to the adventurer in his maturity. Even Titian's brush has not worked with greater richness and freedom, with an effect broader or more entirely legitimate than in the head with its softly flowing beard and the magnificent yet not too ornate robe and vest of plum-coloured velvet and satin.

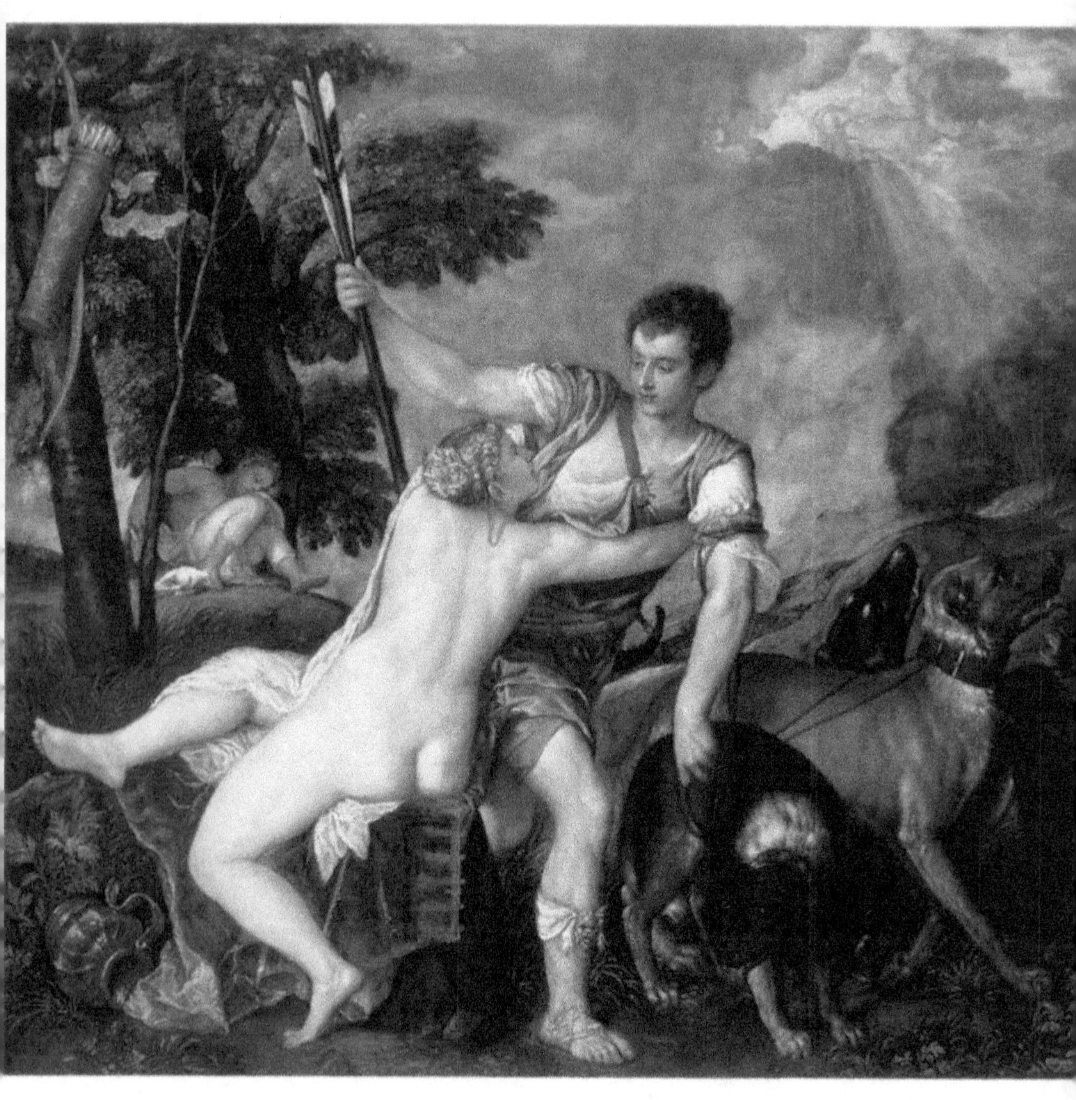

Titian, Venus and Adonis, 1550, Ashmolean, Oxford

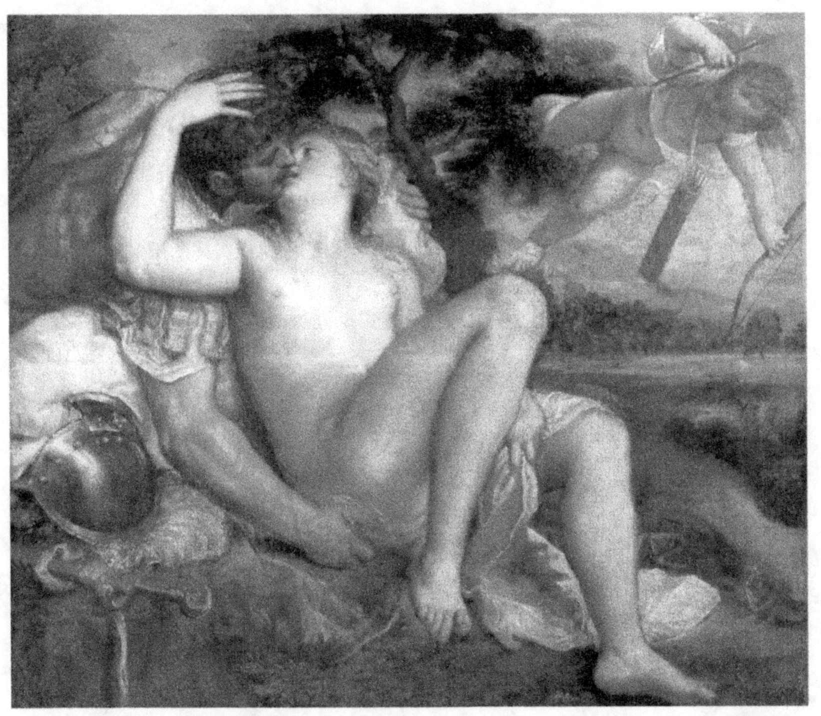

Titian, Venus and Mars and Amor, 1530, Vienna

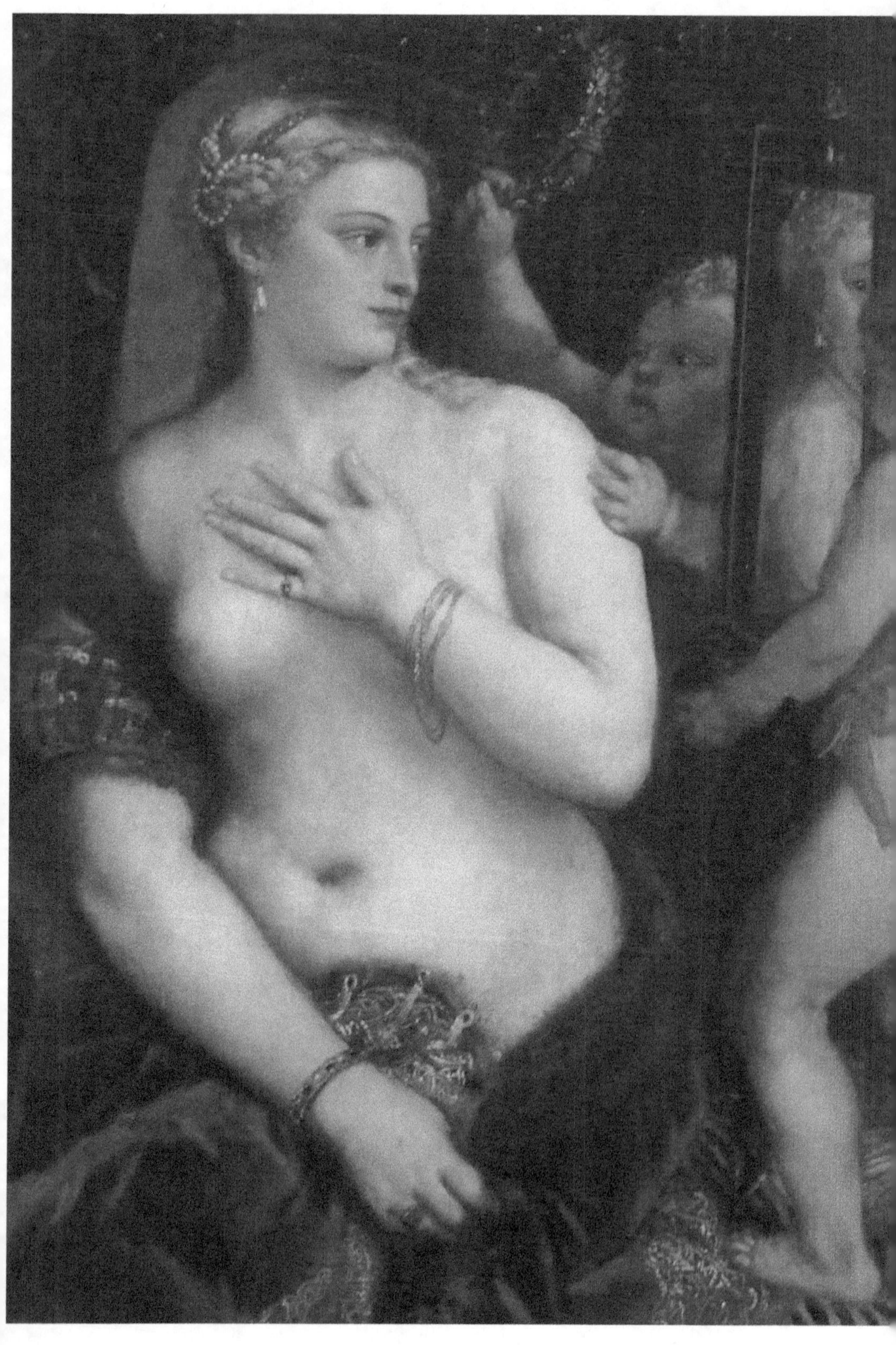

Titian, Venus With a Mirror, 1554-55, Washington, DC

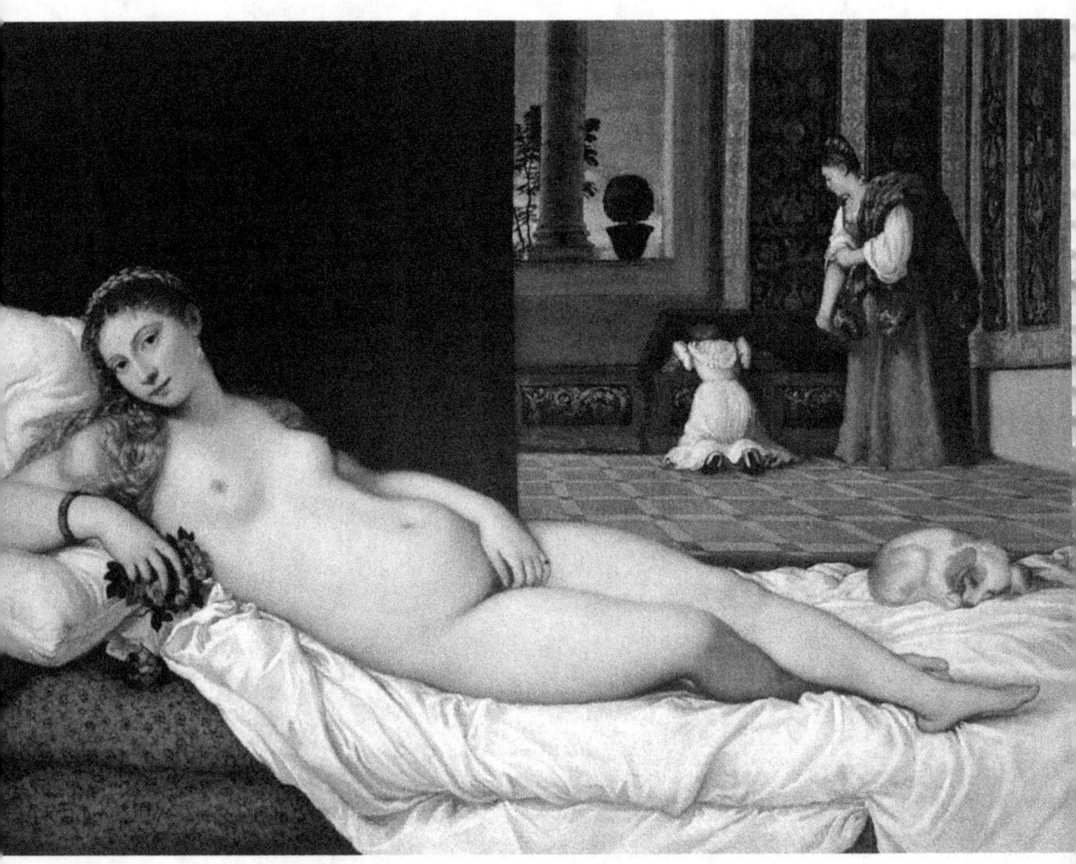

Titian, The Venus of Urbino, 1538, Uffizi, Florence

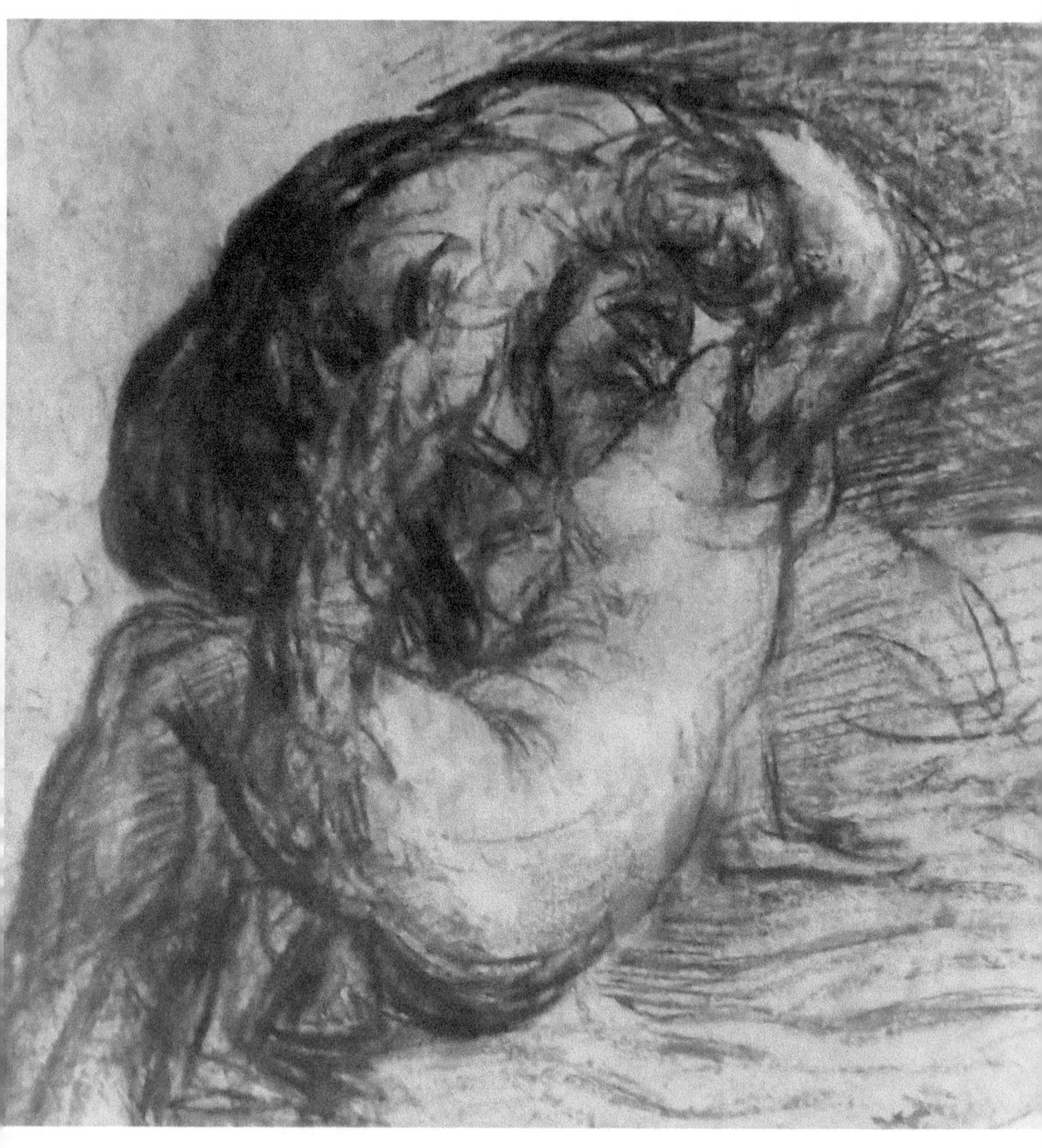

Titian, A Couple, c. 1570, Cambridge

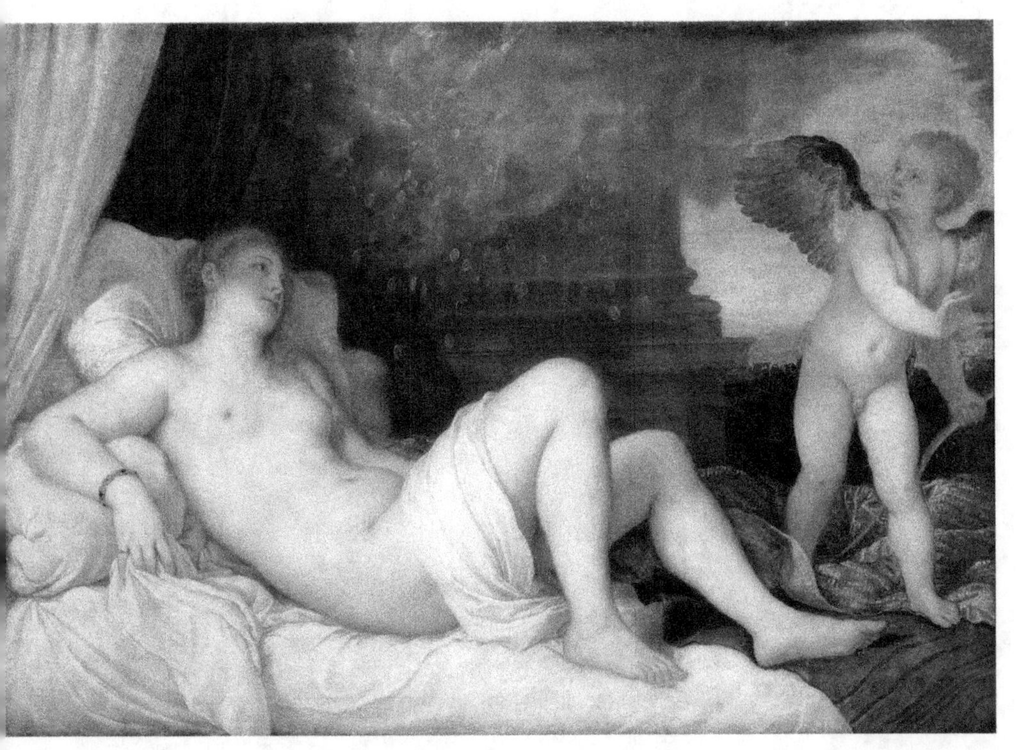

Titian, Danaë, 1544, Naples

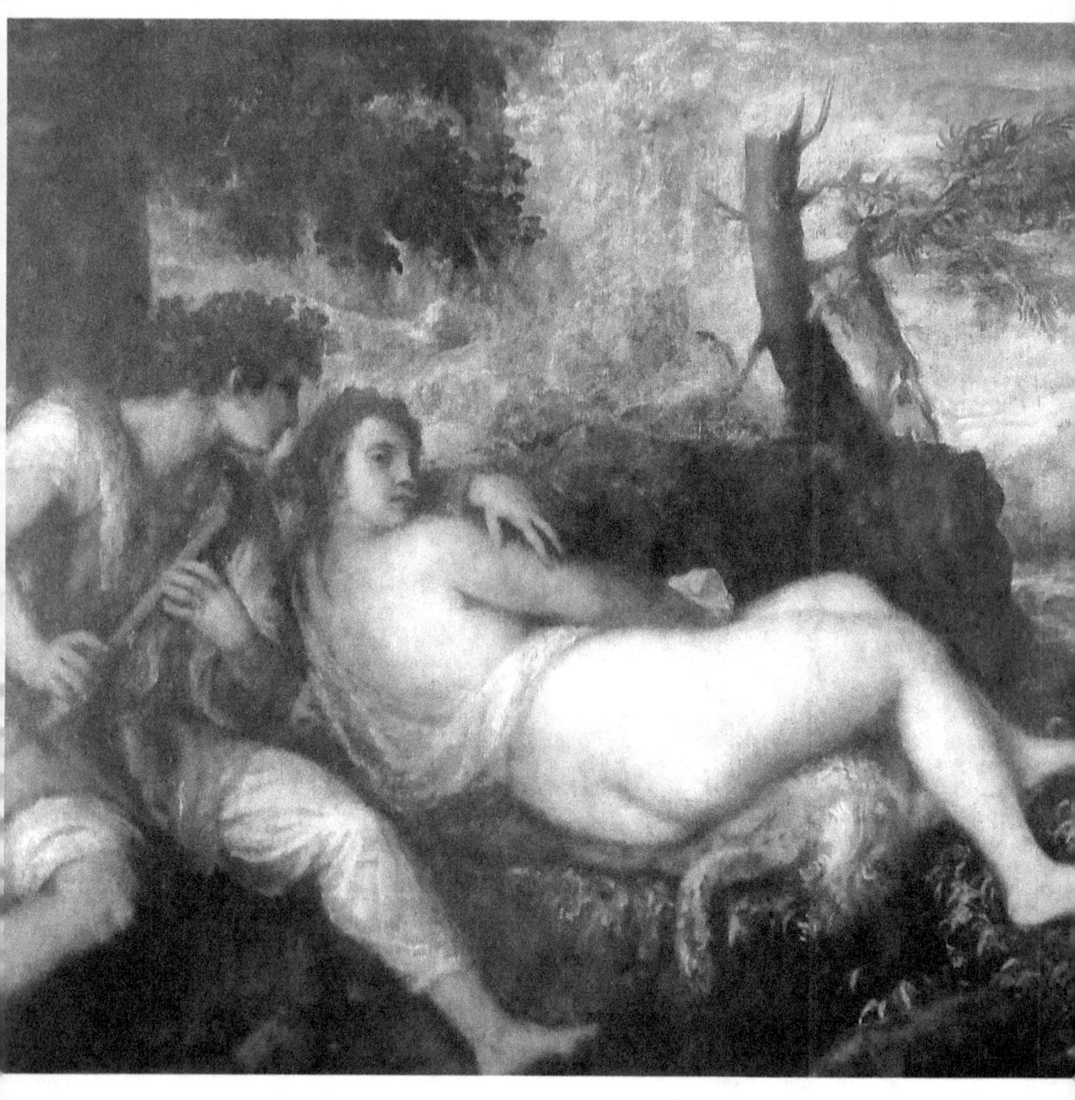

Titian, Nymph and Shepherd, 1575, Vienna

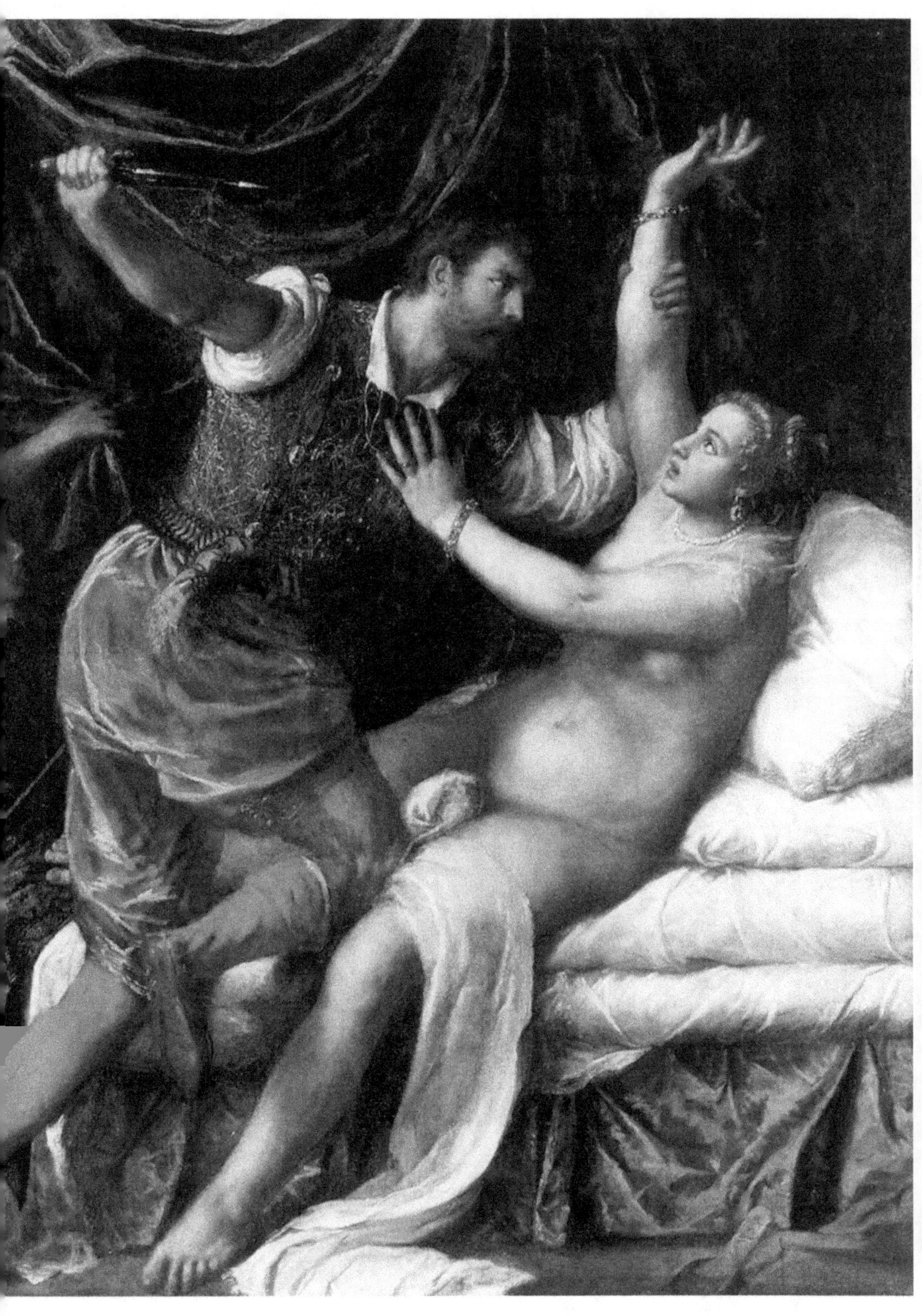

Titian, Tarquin and Lucretia, 1568-71, Cambridge

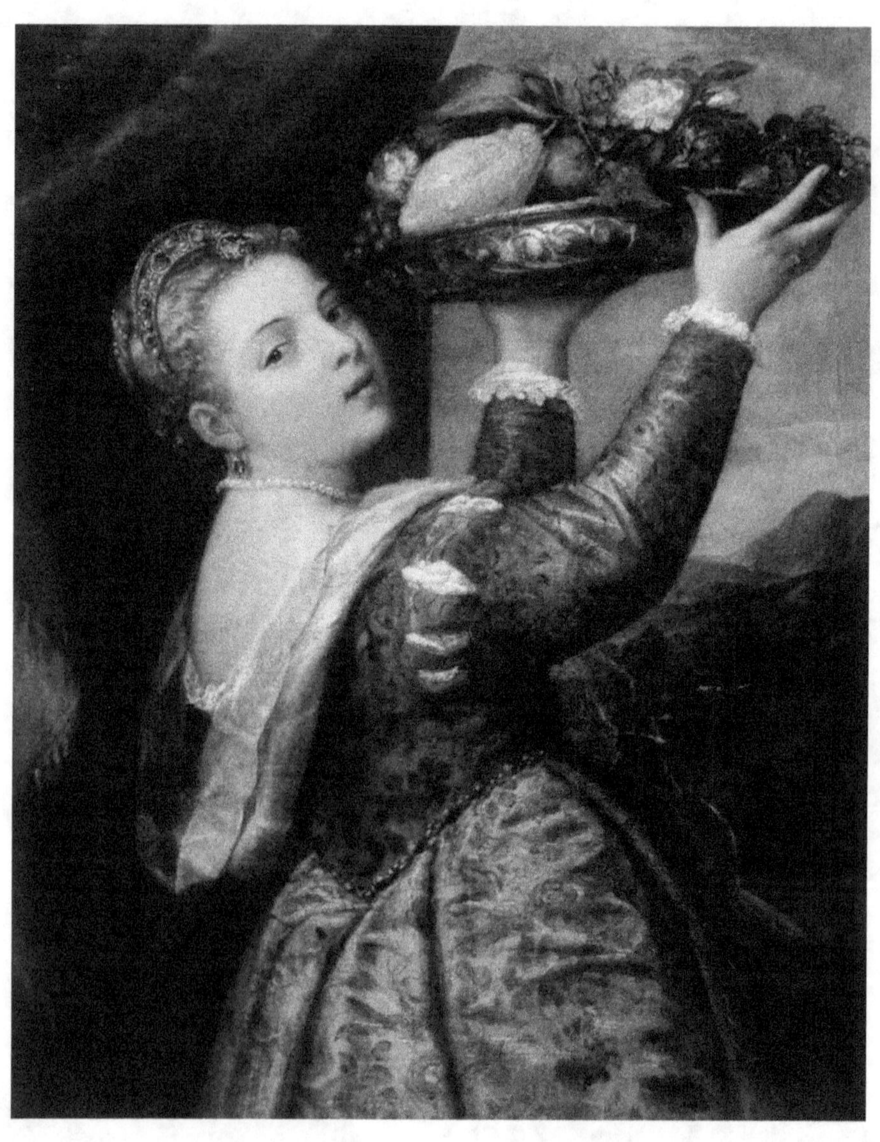

Titian, Girl With a Platter of Fruit, c. 1555, Berlin

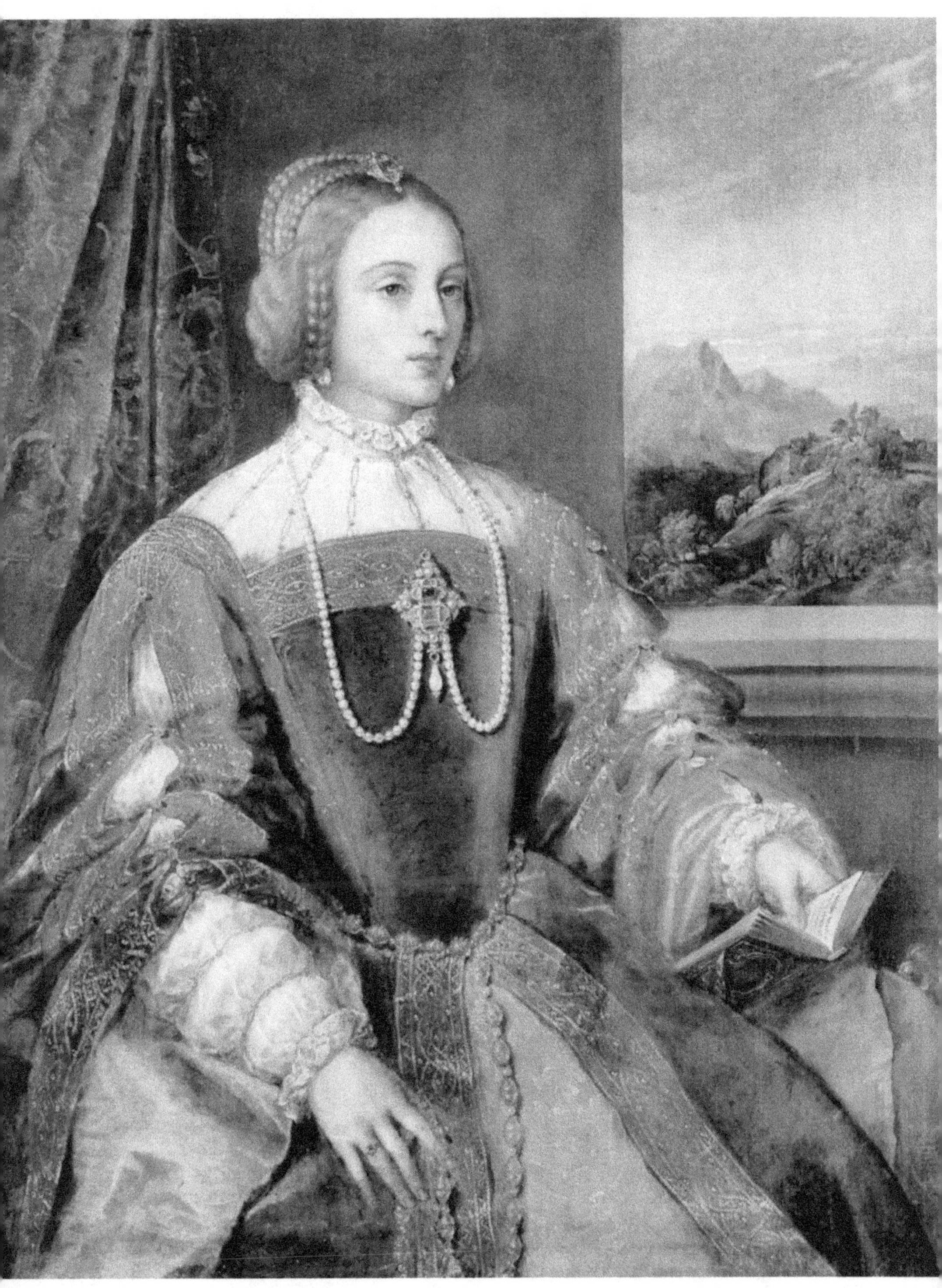

Titian, Portrait of Isabella of Portugal, 1548, Prado

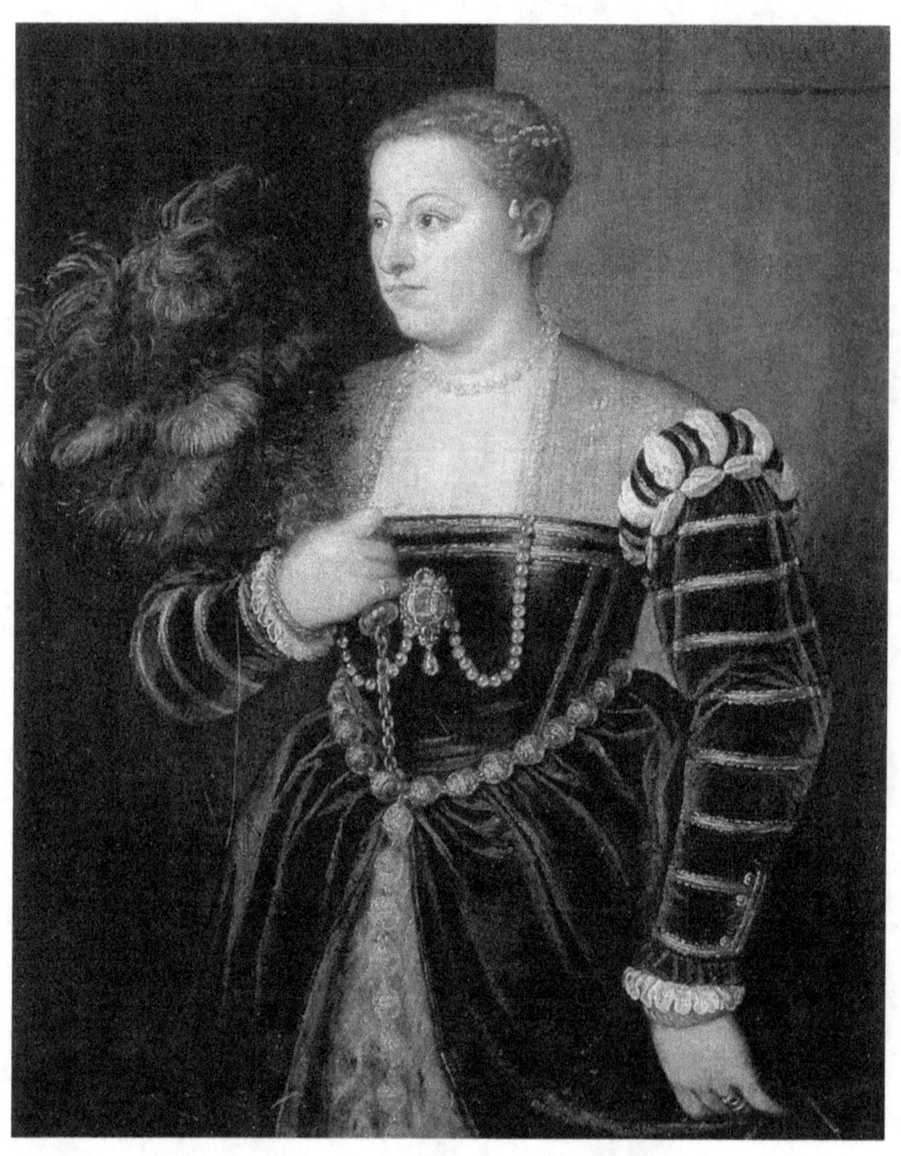

Titian, Lavinia, 1560-65

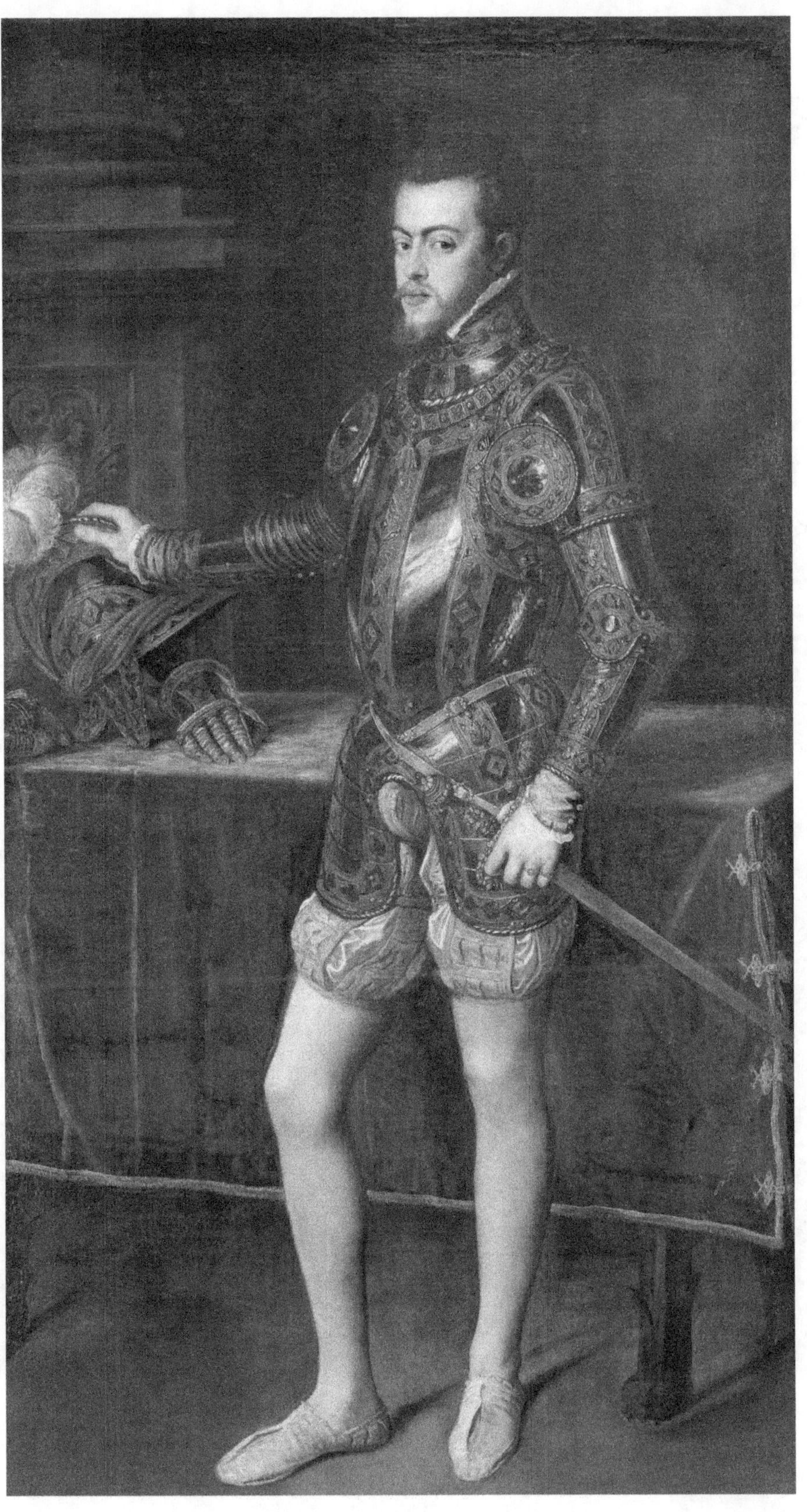

Titian, Philip II, 1551, Prado, Madrid

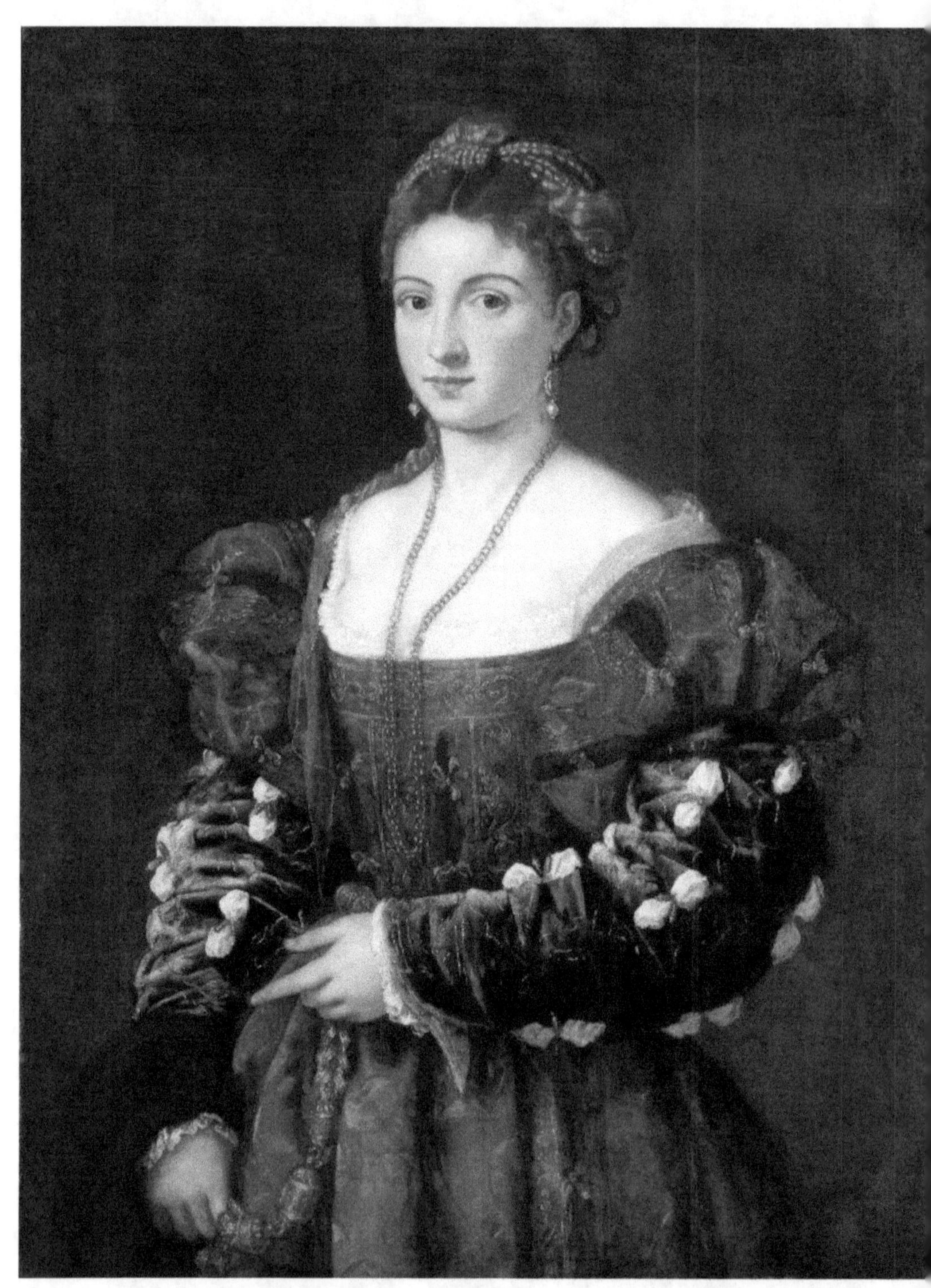

Titian, The Bella, 1536, Pitti Palace

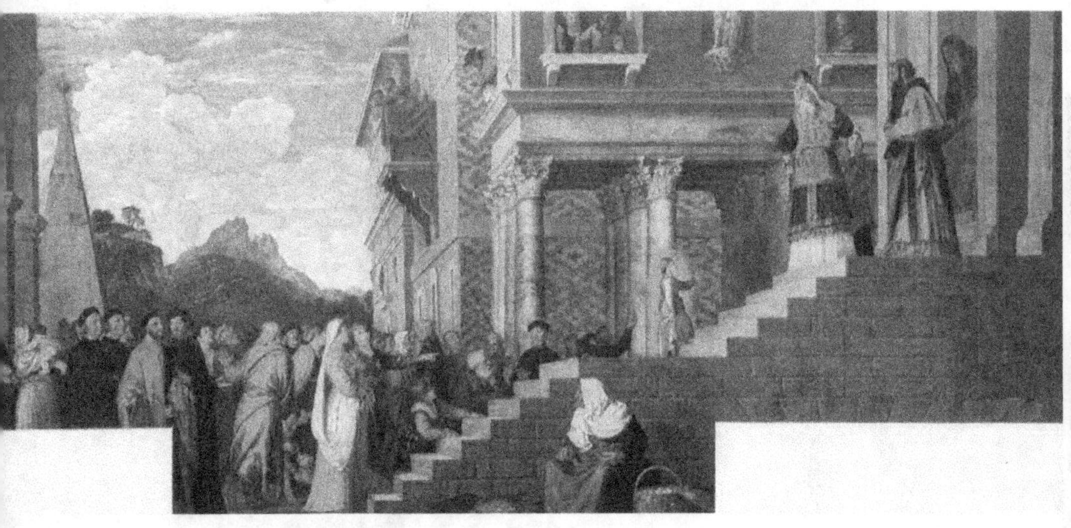

Titian, The Presentation of the Virgin, 1534-38, Venice

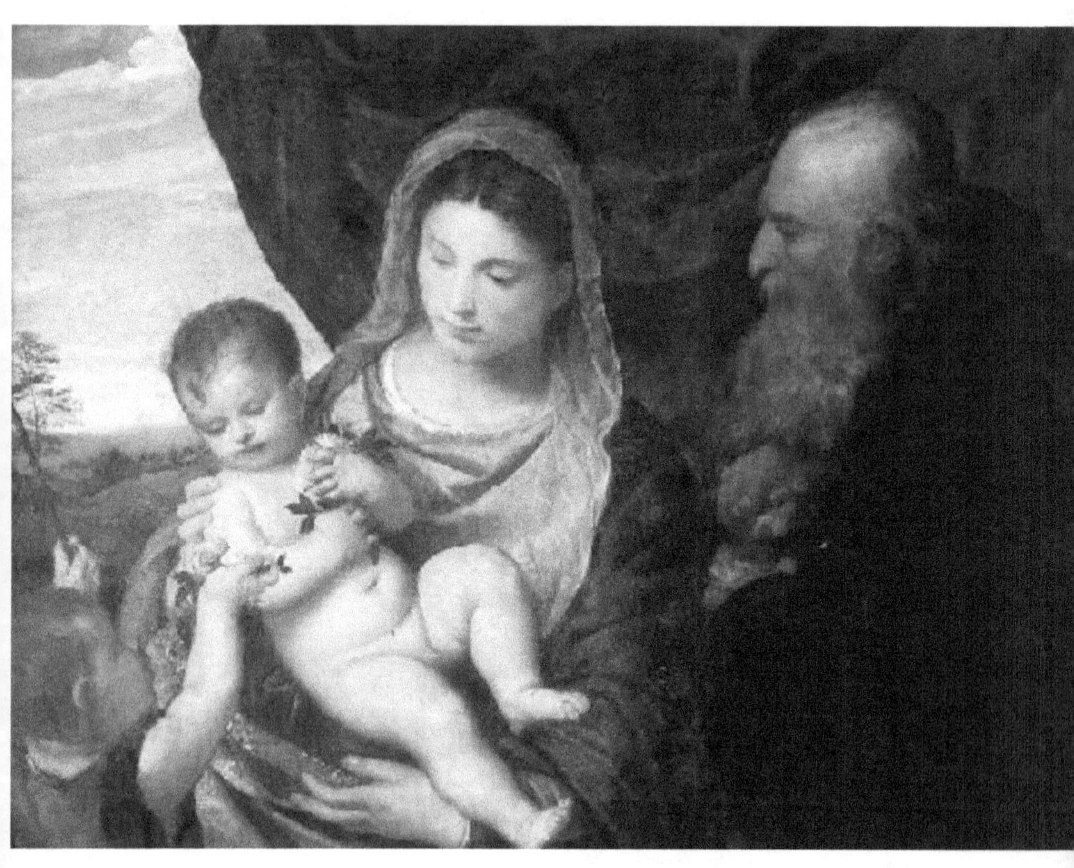

Titian, The Holy Family, 1530s, Uffizi

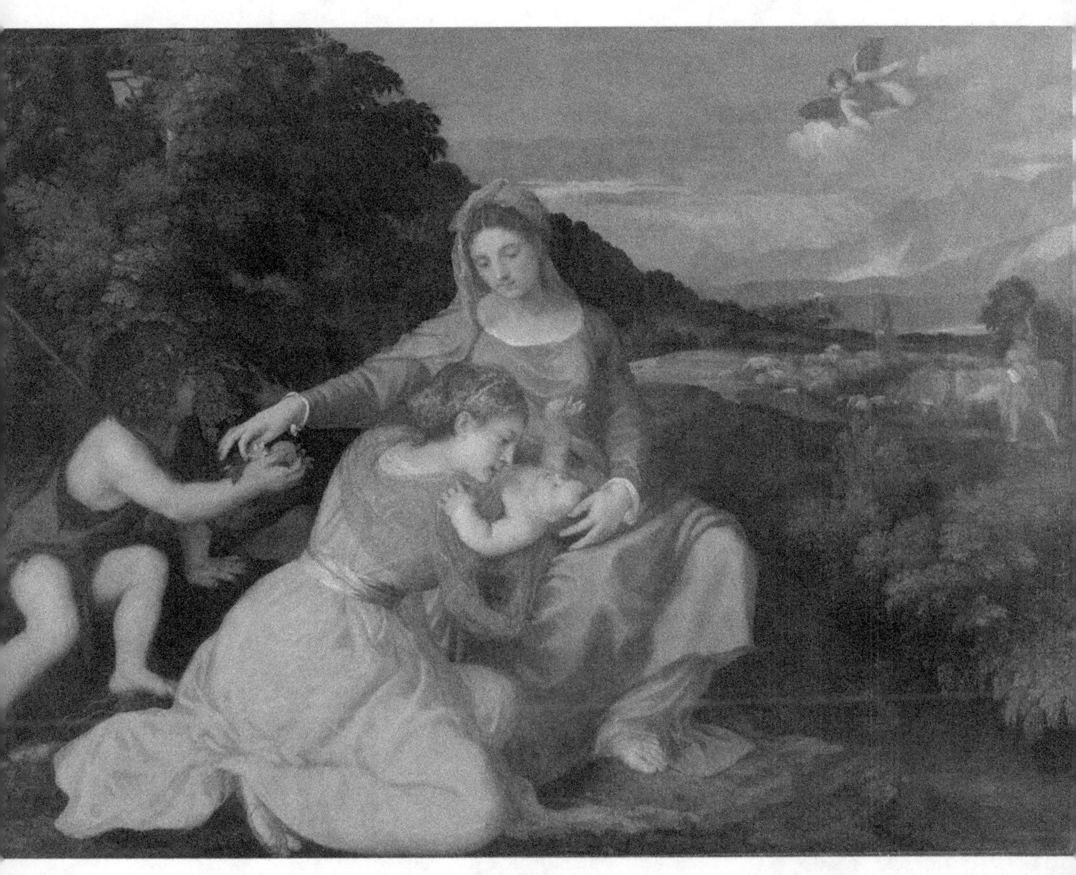

Titian, The Aldobrandini Madonna, National Gallery, London

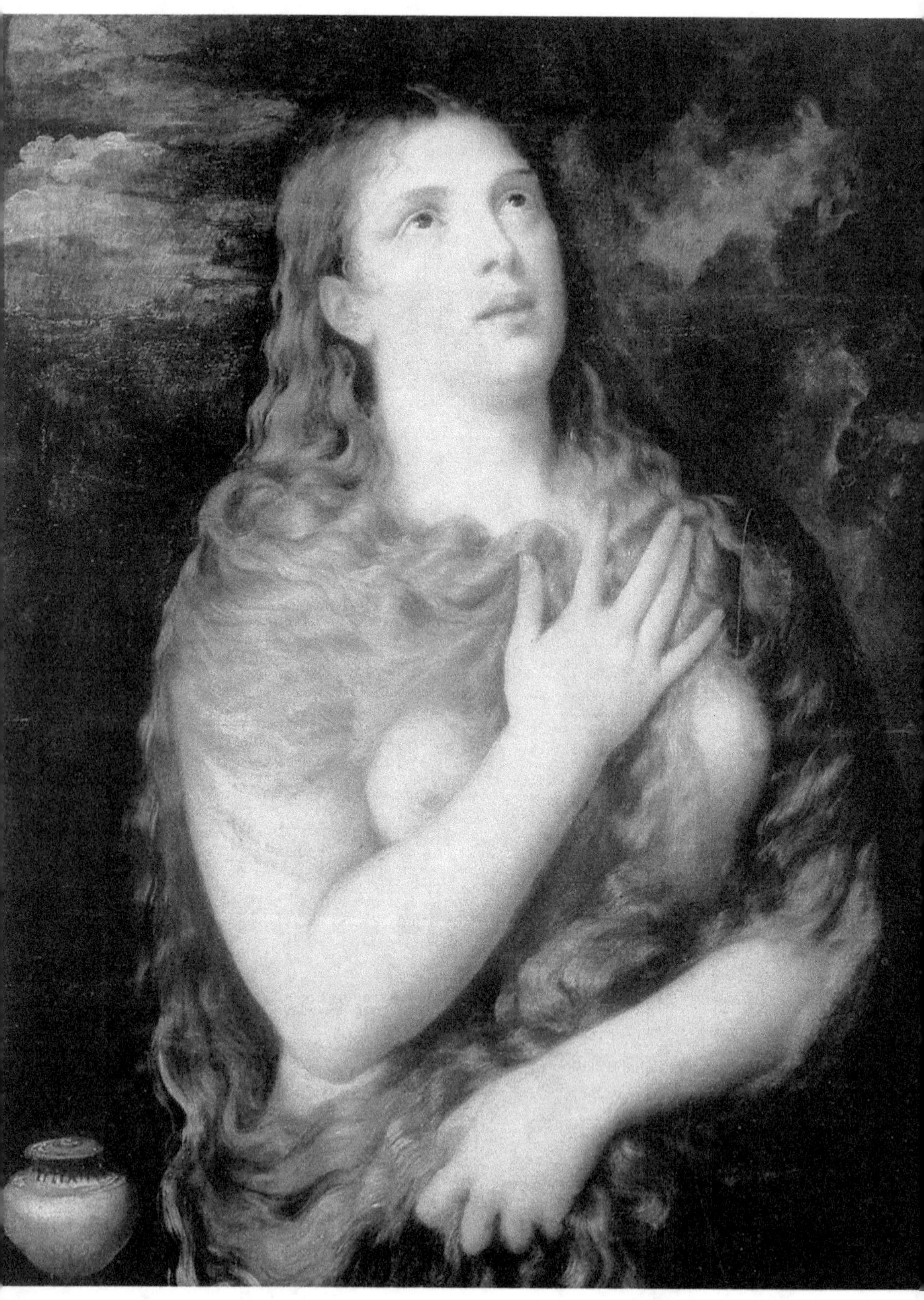

Titian, Mary Magdalene, 1533, Pittit Palace, Florence

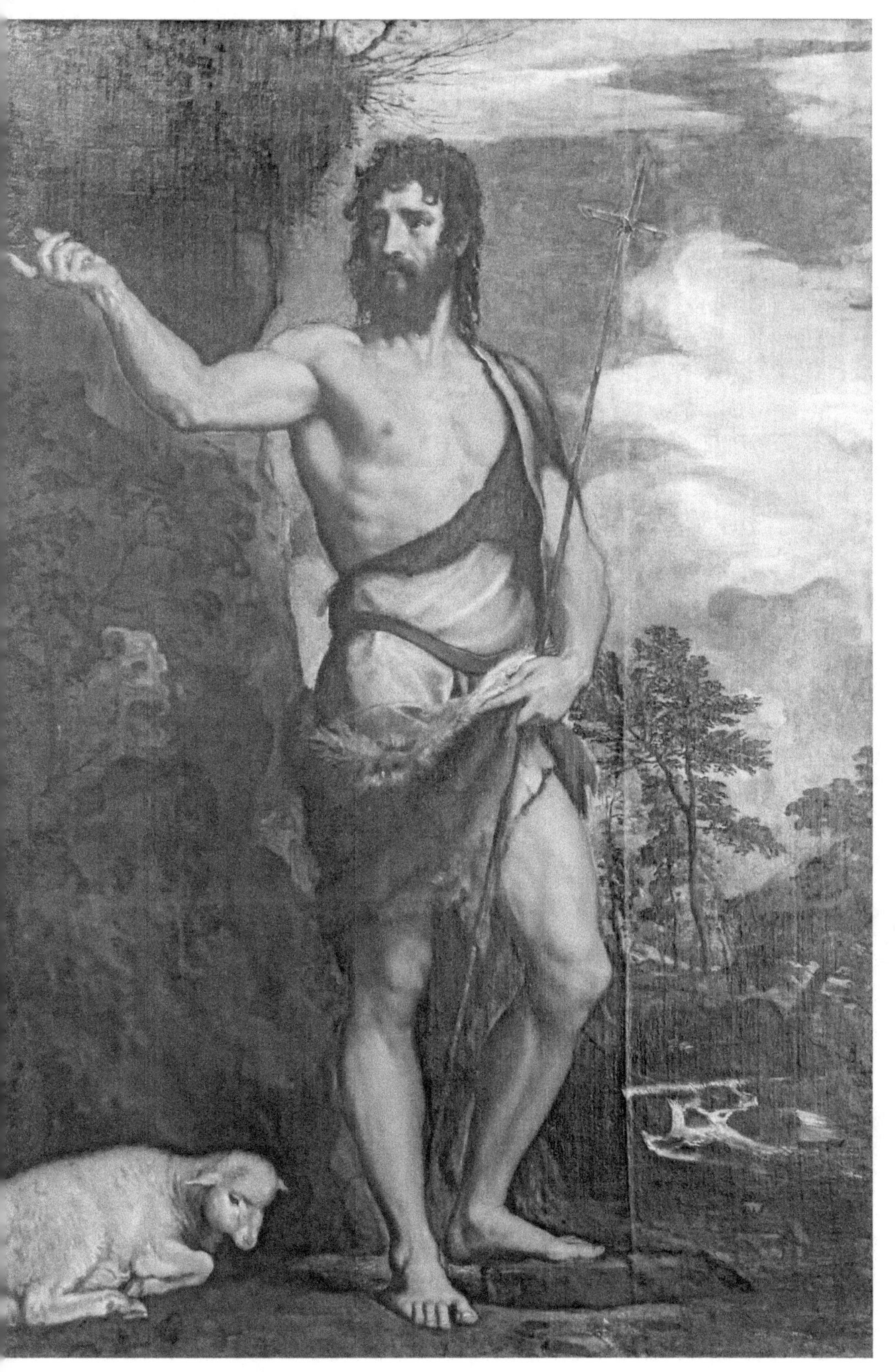

Titian, John the Baptist, 1542, Venice

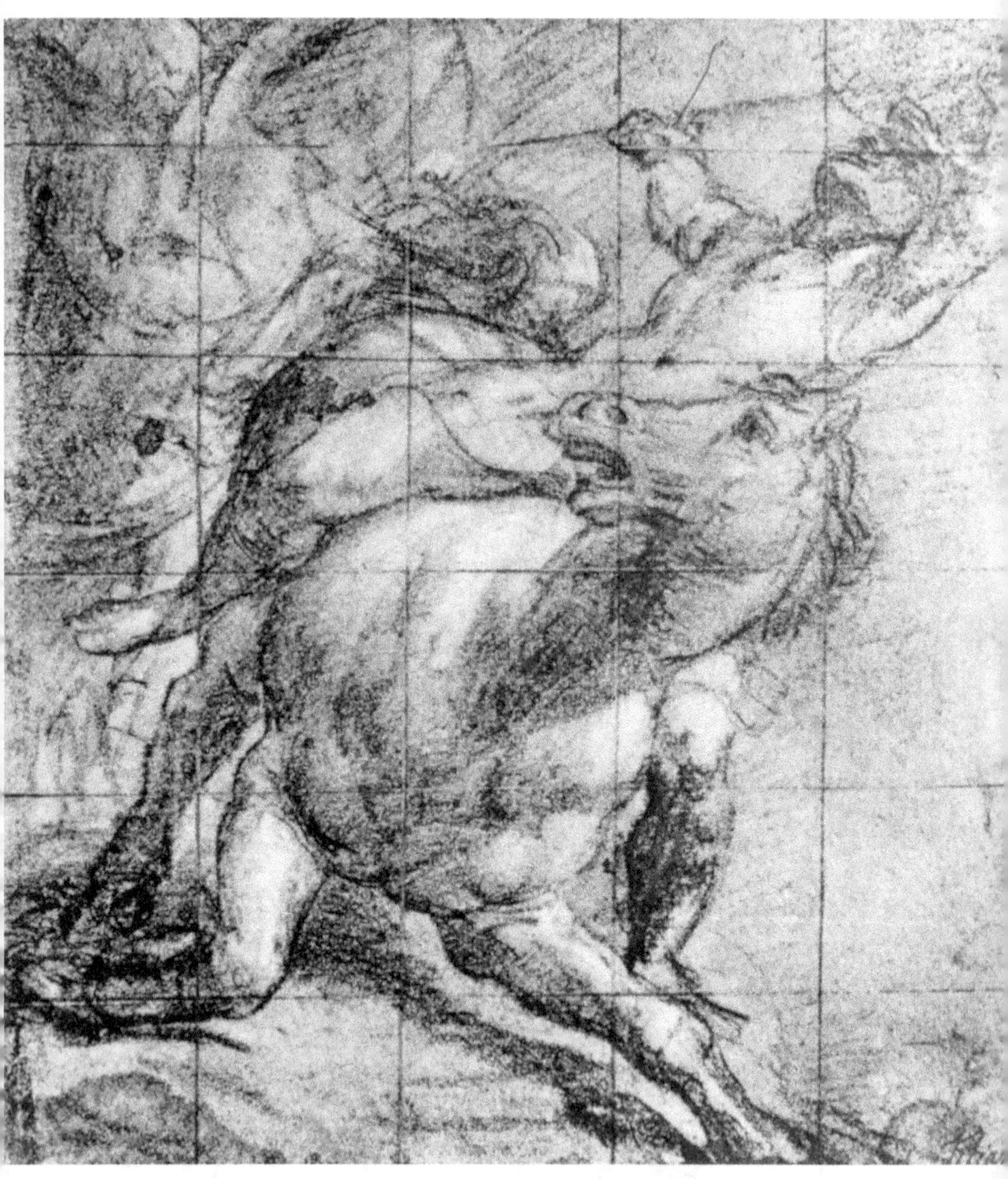

Titian, Studio per cavallo e cavaliere, 1537, Ashmolean Museum, Oxford

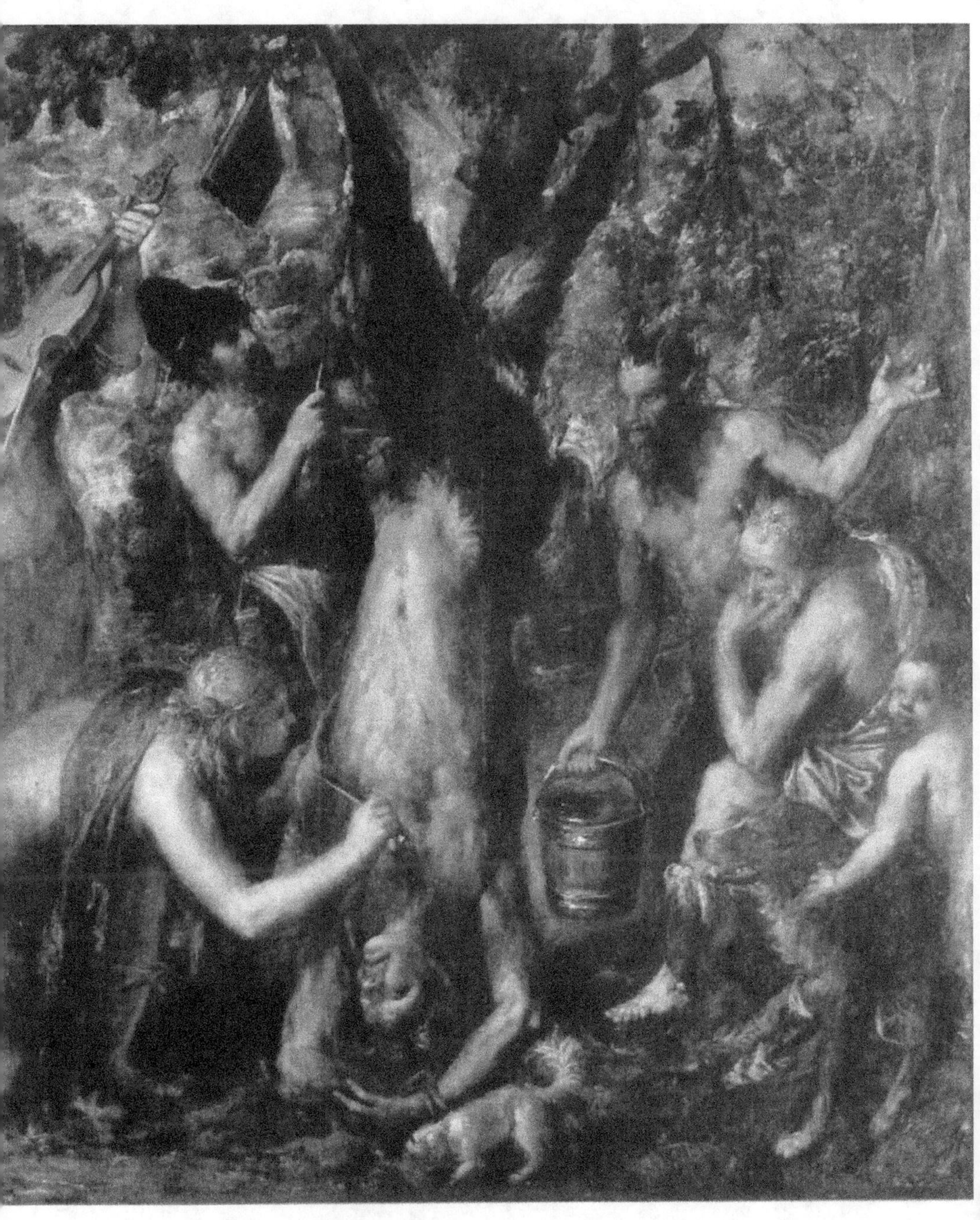

Titian, The Flaying of Marsyas, c. 1570-76, Kromeriz,

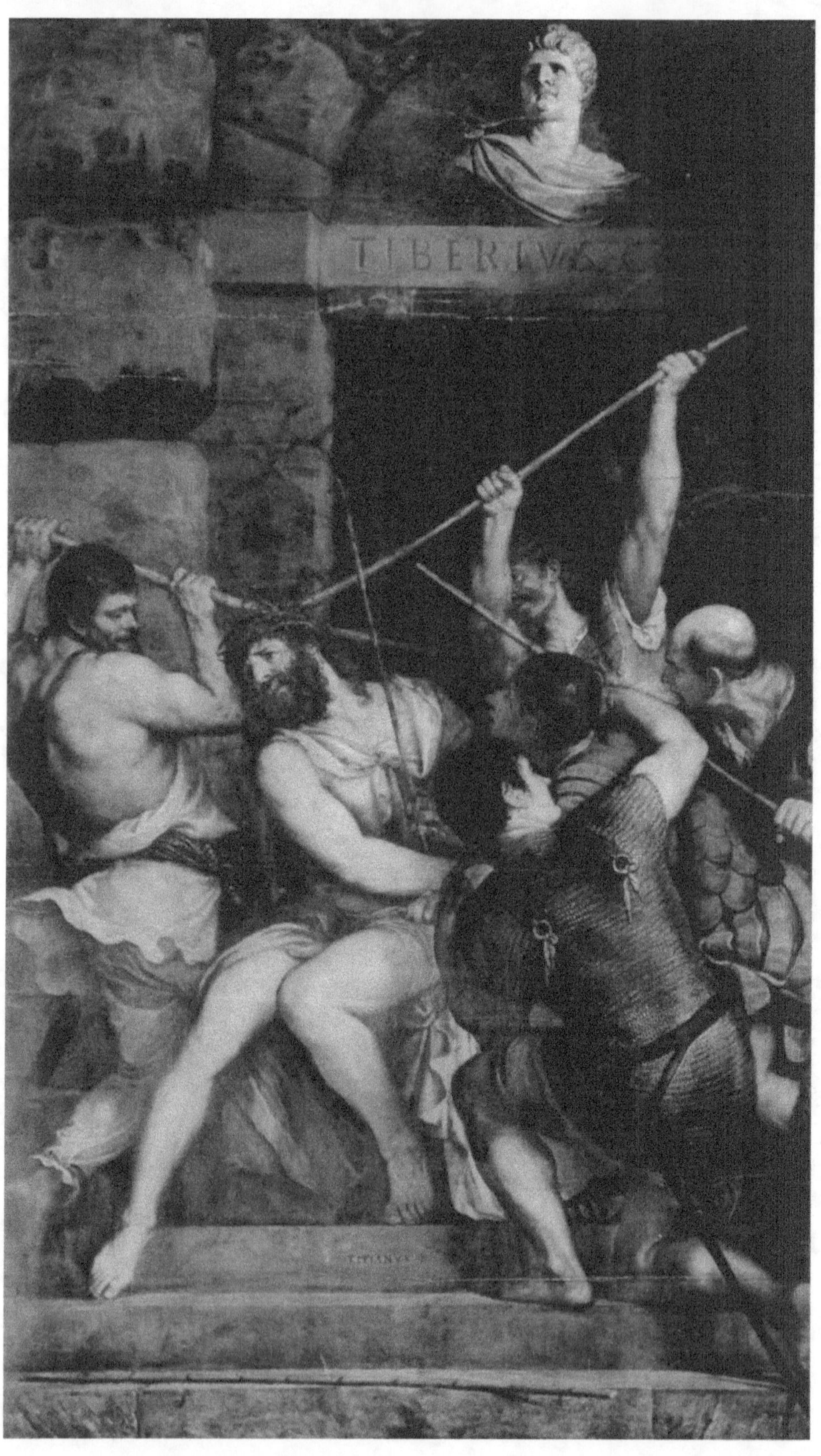

Titian, The Crowning With Thorns, 1572-76, Munich

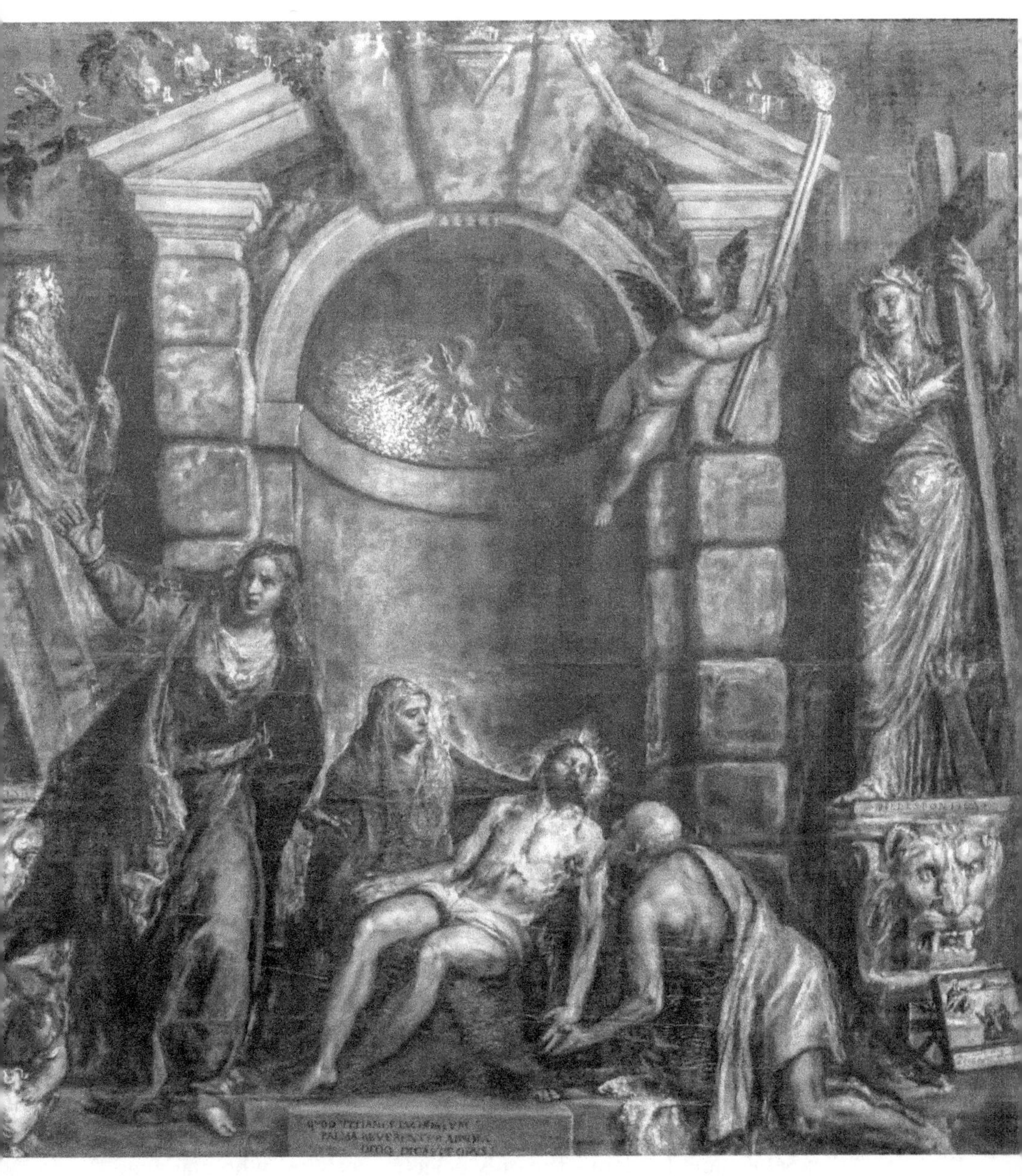

Titian, Pietà, 1576, Venice

CHAPTER III

At last, in the autumn of 1545, the master of Cadore, at the age of sixty-eight years, was to see Rome, its ruins, its statues, its antiquities, and what to the painter of the Renaissance must have meant infinitely more, the Sixtine Chapel and the Stanze of the Vatican. Upon nothing in the history of Venetian art have its lovers, and the many who, with profound interest, trace Titian's noble and perfectly consistent career from its commencement to its close, more reason to congratulate themselves than on this circumstance, that in youth and earlier manhood fortune and his own success kept him from visiting Rome. Though his was not the eclectic tendency, the easily impressionable artistic temperament of a Sebastiano Luciani – the only eclectic, perhaps, who managed all the same to prove and to maintain himself an artist of the very first rank – if Titian had in earlier life been lured to the Eternal City, and had there settled, the glamour of the grand style might have permanently and fatally disturbed his balance. Now it was too late for the splendid and gracious master, who even at sixty-eight had still before him nearly thirty fruitful years, to receive any impressions sufficiently deep to penetrate to the root of his art. There is some evidence to show that Titian, deeply impressed with the highest manifestations of the Florentine and Umbro-Florentine art transplanted to Rome, considered that his work had improved after the visit of 1545-1546. If there was such improvement – and certainly in the ultimate phases of his practice there will be evident in some ways a wider view, a higher grasp of essentials, a more responsive sensitiveness in the conceiving anew of the great sacred subjects – it must have come, not from any effort to assimilate the manner or to assume the standpoint which had obtained in Rome, but from the closer contact with a world which at its centre was beginning to take a deeper, a more solemn and gloomy view of religion and life. It should not be forgotten that this was the year when the great Council of Trent first met, and that during the next twenty years or more the whole of Italy, nay, the whole of the Catholic world, was overshadowed by its deliberations.

Titian's friend and patron of that time, Guidobaldo II., Duke of Urbino, had at first opposed Titian's visit to the Roman court, striving to reserve to himself the services of the Venetian master until such time as he should have carried out for him the commissions with which he was charged. Yielding, however, to the inevitable, and yielding, too, with a good grace, he himself escorted his favourite with his son Orazio from Venice through Ferrara to Pesaro, and having detained him a short while there, granted him an escort through the Papal States to Rome. There he was well received by the Farnese Pope, and with much cordiality by Cardinal Bembo. Rooms were accorded to him in the Belvedere section of the Vatican Palace, and there no doubt he painted the unfinished portrait-group *Paul III. with Cardinal*

Alessandro Farnese and Ottavio Farnese, which has been already described, and with it other pieces of the same type, and portraits of the Farnese family and circle now no longer to be traced. Vasari, well pleased no doubt to renew his acquaintance with the acknowledged head of the contemporary Venetian painters, acted as his cicerone in the visits to the antiquities of Rome, to the statues and art-treasures of the Vatican, while Titian's fellow-citizen Sebastiano del Piombo was in his company when he studied the Stanze of Raphael.

It was but three years since Michelangelo's *Last Judgment* had been uncovered in the Sixtine, and it would have been in the highest degree interesting to read his comments on this gigantic performance, towards which it was so little likely that his sympathies would spontaneously go out. Memorable is the visit paid by Buonarroti, with an unwonted regard for ceremonious courtesy, to Titian in his apartments at the Belvedere, as it is recalled by Vasari with that naïve touch, that power of suggestion, which gives such delightful colour to his unstudied prose. No *Imaginary Conversation* among those that Walter Savage Landor has devised equals in significance this meeting of the two greatest masters then living, simply as it is sketched in by the Aretine biographer. The noble Venetian representing the alternating radiance and gloom of earth, its fairest pages as they unfold themselves, the joys and sorrows, the teeming life of humanity; the mighty Florentine disdainful of the world, its colours, its pulsations, its pomps and vanities, incurious of mankind save in its great symbolical figures, soaring like the solitary eagle into an atmosphere of his own where the dejected beholder can scarce breathe, and, sick at heart, oppressed with awe, lags far behind!

Titian the gracious, the serene, who throughout a long life of splendid and by comparison effortless achievement has openly and candidly drunk deep of all the joys of life, a man even as others are! Michelangelo the austere, the scornful, to whom the pleasures of the world, the company in well-earned leisure of his fellow-man, suggest but the loss of precious hours which might be devoted to the shaping in solitude of masterpieces; in the very depths of whose nature lurk nevertheless, even in old age, the strangest ardours, the fiercest and most insatiate longings for love and friendship!

Let Vasari himself be heard as to this meeting. "Michelangelo and Vasari going one day to pay a visit to Titian in the Belvedere, saw, in a picture which he had then advanced towards completion, a nude female figure representing *Danaë* as she receives the embrace of Jove transformed into a rain of gold, and, as the fashion is in people's presence, praised it much to him. When they had taken leave, and the discussion was as to the art of Titian, Buonarroti praised it highly, saying that the colour and handling pleased him much, but that it was a subject for regret that at Venice they did not learn from the very beginning to design correctly, and that its painters did not follow a better method in their study of art." It is the battle that will so often be renewed between the artist who looks upon colour as merely a complement and adjunct to design, and the painter who regards it as not only the outer covering, but the body and soul of art. We remember how the stiff-necked Ingres, the greatest Raphaelesque of this century, hurled at Delacroix's head the famous dictum, "Le dessin c'est la probité de l'art," and how his illustrious rival, the chief of a romanticism which he would hardly acknowledge, vindicated by works rather than by words his contention that, if design was indeed art's conscience, colour was its life-blood, its very being.

The *Danaë*, seen and admired with reservations by Buonarroti in the painting-room of Titian at the Belvedere, is now, with its beauty diminished in important particulars, to be found with the rest of the Farnese pictures in the gallery of the Naples Museum. It serves to show that if the artist was far beyond the stage of imitation or even of assimilation on the larger scale, he was, at any rate, affected by the Roman atmosphere in art. For once he here comes nearer to the realisation of Tintoretto's ideal – the colour of Titian and the design of Michelangelo – than his impetuous pupil and rival ever did. While preserving in the *Danaë* his own true warmth and transparency of Venetian colour – now somewhat obscured yet not effaced – he combines unusual weightiness and majesty with voluptuousness in the nude, and successfully strives after a more studied rhythm in the harmony of the composition generally than the art of Venice usually affected.

Titian, in his return from Rome, which he was never to revisit, made a stay at Florence with an eye, as we may guess, both to business and pleasure. There, as Vasari takes care to record, our master visited the artistic sights, and *rimase stupefatto* – remained in breathless astonishment – as he had done when he made himself acquainted with the artistic glories of Rome. This is but vague, and a little too much smacks of self-flattery and adulation of the brother Tuscans. Titian was received by Duke Cosimo at Poggio a Caiano, but his offer to paint the portrait of the Medici ruler was not well received. It may be, as Vasari surmises, that this attitude was taken up by the duke in order not to do wrong to the "many noble craftsmen" then practising in his city and dominion. More probably, however, Cosimo's hatred and contempt of his father's minion Aretino, whose portrait by Titian he had condescended to retain, yet declined to acknowledge, impelled him to show something less than favour to the man who was known to be the closest friend and intimate of this self-styled "Scourge of Princes."

Crowe and Cavalcaselle have placed about the year 1555 the extravagantly lauded *St. John the Baptist in the Desert*, once in the church of S.M. Maria Maggiore at Venice, and now in the Accademia there. To the writer it appears that it would best come in at this stage – that is to say in or about 1545 – not only because the firm close handling in the nude would be less explicable ten years later on, but because the conception of the majestic St. John is for once not pictorial but purely sculptural. Leaving Rome, and immediately afterwards coming into contact for the first time with the wonders of the earlier Florentine art, Titian might well have conceived, might well have painted thus. Strange to say, the influence is not that of Michelangelo, but, unless the writer is greatly deceived, that of Donatello, whose noble ascetic type of the *Precursor* is here modernised, and in the process deprived of some of its austerity. The glorious mountain landscape, with its brawling stream, fresher and truer than any torrent of Ruysdael's, is all Titian. It makes the striking figure of St. John, for all its majesty, appear not a little artificial.

The little town of Serravalle, still so captivatingly Venetian in its general aspect, holds one of the most magnificent works of Titian's late time, a vast *Virgin and Child with St. Peter and St. Andrew*. This hangs – or did when last seen by the writer – in the choir of the Church of St. Andrew; there is evidence in Titian's correspondence that it was finished in 1547, so that it must have been undertaken soon after the return from Rome. In the distance between the two majestic figures of the saints is a prospect of landscape with a lake, upon which Titian has shown on a reduced scale Christ calling Peter and Andrew from their nets; an undisguised adaptation this, by the veteran master, of the divine Urbinate's *Miraculous Draught of Fishes*, but one which made of the borrowed motive a new thing, no excrescence but an integral part of the conception. In this great work, which to be more universally celebrated requires only to be better known to those who do not come within the narrow circle of students, there is evidence that while Titian, after his stay at the Papal court, remained firm as a rock in his style and general principles – luckily a Venetian and no pseudo-Roman, – his imagination became more intense in its glow, gloomier but grander, than it had been in middle age – his horizon altogether vaster. To a grand if sometimes too unruffled placidity succeeded a physical and psychical perturbation which belonged both to the man in advanced years and to the particular moment in the century. Even in his treatment of classic myth, of the nude in goddess and woman, there was, as we shall see presently, a greater unrest and a more poignant sensuality – there was evidence of a mind and temperament troubled anew instead of being tranquillised by the oncoming of old age.

Are we to place here, as Crowe and Cavalcaselle do, the *Venus and Cupid* of the Tribuna and the *Venus with the Organ Player* of the Prado? The technical execution of these canvases, the treatment of landscape in the former, would lead the writer to place them some years farther on still in the *oeuvre* of the master. There are, however, certain reasons for following them in this chronological arrangement. The *Venus and Cupid* which hangs in the Tribuna of the Uffizi, as the pendant to the more resplendent but more realistic *Venus of Urbino*, is a darker and less well-preserved picture than its present companion, but a grander if a more audacious presentment of the love-goddess. Yet even here she is not so much the Cytherean as an embodiment of the Venetian ideal of the later time, an exemplification of the undisguised worship of fleshly loveliness which then existed in Venice. It has been pointed out that the later Venus has the features of Titian's fair daughter Lavinia, and this is no doubt to a certain extent true. The goddesses, nymphs, and women of this time bear a sort of general family resemblance to her and to each other. This piece illustrates the preferred type of Titian's old age, as the *Vanitas, Herodias,* and *Flora* illustrate the preferred type of his youth; as the paintings which we have learnt to associate with the Duchess of Urbino illustrate that of his middle time. The dignity and rhythmic outline of Eros in the *Danaë* of Naples have been given up in favour of a more naturalistic conception of the insinuating urchin, who is in this *Venus and Cupid* the successor of those much earlier *amorini* in the *Worship of Venus* at Madrid. The landscape in its sweeping breadth is very characteristic of the late time, and would give good reason for placing the picture later than it here appears. The difficulty is this. The *Venus with the Organ Player*[*39] of Madrid, which in many essential points is an inferior repetition of the later Venus of the Tribuna, contains the portrait of Ottavio Farnese, much as we see him in the unfinished group painted, as has been recorded, at Rome in 1546. This being the case, it is not easy to place the *Venus and Cupid,* or its subsequent adaptation, much later than just before the journey to Augsburg. The *Venus with the Organ Player* has been overrated; there are things in this canvas which we cannot without offence to Titian ascribe to his own brush. Among these are the tiresome, formal landscape, the wooden little dog petted by Venus, and perhaps some other passages. The goddess herself and the amorous Ottavio, though this last is not a very striking or successful portrait, may perhaps be left to the master. He vindicates himself more completely than in any other passage of the work when he depicts the youthful, supple form of the Venetian courtesan, as in a merely passive pose she personates the goddess whose insignificant votary she really is. It cannot be denied that he touches here the lowest level reached by him in such delineations. What offends in this *Venus with the Organ Player*, or rather *Ottavio Farnese with his Beloved*, is that its informing sentiment is not love, or indeed any community of sentiment, but an ostentatious pride in the possession of covetable beauty subdued like that of Danaë herself by gold.

If we are to assume with Crowe and Cavalcaselle that the single figure *Ecce Homo* of the Prado Gallery was the piece taken by the master to Charles V. when, at the bidding of the Emperor, he journeyed to Augsburg, we can only conclude that his design was carried out by pupils or assistants. The execution is not such as we can ascribe to the brush which is so shortly to realise for the monarch a group of masterpieces.

It was in January 1548 that Titian set forth to obey the command of the Emperor, "per far qualche opera," as Count Girolamo della Torre has it in a letter of recommendation given to Titian for the Cardinal of Trent at Augsburg. It is significant to find the writer mentioning the painter, not by any of the styles and titles which he had a right to bear, especially at the court of Charles V., but extolling him as "Messer Titiano Pittore et il primo huomo della Christianita."[*40]

It might be imagined that it would be a terrible wrench for Titian, at the age of seventy, to transplant himself suddenly, and for the first time, into a foreign land. But then he was not as other men of seventy are. The final years of his unexampled career will conclusively show that he preserved his mental and physical vigour to the end. Further, the imperial court with its Spanish etiquette, its Spanish language and manners, was much the same at Augsburg as he had known it on previous occasions at Bologna. Moreover, Augsburg and Nuremberg[*41] had, during the last fifty years, been in close touch with Venice in all matters appertaining to art and commerce. Especially the great banking house of the Fuggers had the most intimate relations with the queen-city of the Adriatic. Yet art of the two great German cities would doubtless appeal less to the Venetian who had arrived at the zenith of his development than it would and did to the Bellinis and their school at the beginning of the century. The gulf had become a far wider one, and the points of contact were fewer.

The trusted Orazio had been left behind, notwithstanding the success which he had achieved during the Roman tour, and it may be assumed that he presided over the studio and workshop at Biri Grande during his father's absence. Titian was accompanied to Augsburg by his second cousin, Cesare Vecellio,[*42] who no doubt had a minor share in very many of the canvases belonging to the period of residence at Augsburg. Our master's first and most grateful task must have been the painting of the great equestrian portrait of the Emperor at the Battle of Mühlberg, which now hangs in the Long Gallery of the Prado at Madrid. It suffered much injury in the fire of the Pardo Palace, which annihilated so many masterpieces, but is yet very far from being the "wreck" which, with an exaggeration not easily pardonable under the circumstances, Crowe and Cavalcaselle have described it. In the presence of one of the world's masterpieces criticism may for once remain silent, willingly renouncing all its rights. No purpose would be served here by recording how much paint has been abraded in one corner, how much added in another. A deep sense of thankfulness should possess us that the highest manifestation of Titian's genius has been preserved, even though it be shorn of some of its original beauty. Splendidly armed in steel from head to foot, and holding firmly grasped in his hand the spear, emblem of command in this instance rather than of combat, Cæsar advances with a mien impassive yet of irresistible domination. He bestrides with ease his splendid dark-brown charger, caparisoned in crimson, and heavily weighted like himself with the full panoply of battle, a perfect harmony being here subtly suggested between man and beast. The rich landscape, with a gleam of the Elbe in the distance, is still in the half gloom of earliest day; but on the horizon, and in the clouds overhead, glows the red ominous light of sunrise, colouring the veils of the morning mist. The Emperor is alone – alone as he must be in life and in death – a man, yet lifted so high above other men that the world stretches far below at his feet, while above him this ruler knows no power but that of God. It is not even the sneer of cold command, but a majesty far higher and more absolutely convinced of its divine origin, that awes the beholder as he gazes. In comparison with the supreme dignity of this ugly, pallid Hapsburger, upon whom disease and death have already laid a shadowy finger, how artificial appear the divine assumptions of an Alexander, how theatrical the Olympian airs of an Augustus, how merely vulgar and ill-worn the imperial poses of a Napoleon.

No veracious biographer of Titian could pretend that he is always thus imaginative, that coming in contact with a commanding human individuality he always thus unfolds the outer wrappings to reveal the soul within. Indeed, especially in the middle time just past, he not infrequently contents himself with the splendid outsides of splendid things. To interpret this masterpiece as the writer has ventured to do, it is not necessary to assume that Titian reasoned out the poetic vision, which was at the same time an absolutely veracious presentment, argument-atively with himself, as the painter of such a portrait in words might have done. Pictorial genius of the creative order does not proceed by such methods, but sees its subject as a whole, leaving to others the task of probing and unravelling. It should be borne in mind, too, that this is the first in order, as it is infinitely the greatest and the most significant among the vast equestrian portraits of monarchs by court painters. Velazquez on the one hand, and Van Dyck on the other, have worked wonders in the same field. Yet their finest productions, even the *Philip IV.*, the *Conde Duque Olivarez*, the *Don Balthasar Carlos* of the Spaniard, even the two equestrian portraits of Charles I., the *Francisco de Moncada*, the *Prince Thomas of Savoy* of the Fleming, are in comparison but magnificent show pieces aiming above all at decorative pomp and an imposing general effect.

We come to earth and every-day weariness again with the full-length of Charles V., which is now in the Alte Pinakothek of Munich. Here the monarch, dressed in black and seated in a well-worn crimson velvet chair, shows without disguise how profoundly he is ravaged by ill-health and *ennui*. Fine as the portrait still appears notwithstanding its bad condition, one feels somehow that Titian is not in this instance, as he is in most others, perfect master of his material, of the main elements of his picture. The problem of relieving the legs cased in black against a relatively light background, and yet allowing to them their full plastic form, is not perfectly solved. Neither is it, by the way, as a rule in the canvases of those admirable painters of men, the quasi-Venetians, Moretto of Brescia and Moroni of Bergamo. The Northerners – among them Holbein and Lucidel – came nearer to perfect success in this particular matter. The splendidly brushed-in prospect of cloudy sky and far-stretching country recalls, as Morelli has observed, the landscapes of Rubens, and suggests that he underwent the influence of the Cadorine in this respect as in many others, especially after his journey as ambassador to Madrid.

Another portrait, dating from the first visit to Augsburg, is the half-length of the Elector John Frederick of Saxony, now in the Imperial Gallery at Vienna. He sits obese and stolid, yet not without the dignity that belongs to absolute simplicity, showing on his left cheek the wound received at the battle of Mühlberg. The picture has, as a portrait by Titian, no very commanding merit, no seduction of technique, and it is easy to imagine that Cesare Vecellio may have had a share in it. Singular is the absence of all pose, of all attempt to harmonise the main lines of the design or give pictorial elegance to the naïve directness of the presentment. This mode of conception may well have been dictated to the courtly Venetian by sturdy John Frederick himself.

The master painted for Mary, Queen Dowager of Hungary, four canvases specially mentioned by Vasari, *Prometheus Bound to the Rock, Ixion, Tantalus,* and *Sisyphus,* which were taken to Spain at the moment of the definitive migration of the court in 1556. Crowe and Cavalcaselle state that the whole four perished in the all-devouring conflagration of the Pardo Palace, and put down the *Prometheus* and *Sisyphus* of the Prado Gallery as copies by Sanchez Coello. It is difficult to form a definite judgment on canvases so badly hung, so darkened and injured. They certainly look much more like Venetian originals than Spanish copies. These mythological subjects may very properly be classed with the all too energetic ceiling-pictures now in the Sacristy of the Salute. Here again the master, in the effort to be grandiose in a style not properly his, overreaches himself and becomes artificial. He must have left Augsburg this time in the autumn of 1548, since in the month of October of that year we find him at Innsbruck making a family picture of the children of King Ferdinand, the Emperor's brother. That monarch himself, his two sons and five daughters, he had already portrayed.

Much feasting, much rejoicing, in the brilliant and jovial circle presided over by Aretino and the brother Triumvirs, followed upon our master's return to Venice. Aretino, who after all was not so much the scourge as the screw of princes, would be sure to think the more highly of the friend whom he really cherished in all sincerity, when he returned from close and confidential intercourse with the mightiest ruler of the age, the source not only of honour but of advantages which the Aretine, like Falstaff, held more covetable because more substantial. To the year 1549 belongs the gigantic woodcut *The Destruction of Pharaoh's Host*, designed, according to the inscription on the print, by "the great and immortal Titian," and engraved by Domenico delle Greche, who, notwithstanding his name, calls himself "depentore Venetiano." He is not, as need hardly be pointed out, to be confounded with the famous Veneto-Spanish painter, Domenico Theotocopuli, Il Greco, whose date of birth is just about this time (1548).

Titian, specially summoned by the Emperor, travelled back to Augsburg in November 1550. Charles had returned thither with Prince Philip, the heir-presumptive of the Spanish throne, and it can hardly be open to question that one of the main objects for which the court painter was made to undertake once more the arduous journey across the Alps was to depict the son upon whom all the monarch's hopes and plans were centred. Charles, whose health had still further declined, was now, under an accumulation of political misfortune, gloomier than ever before, more completely detached from the things of the world. Barely over fifty at this moment, he seemed already, and, in truth, was an old man, while the master of Cadore at seventy-three shone in the splendid autumn of his genius, which even then had not reached its final period of expansion. Titian enjoyed the confidence of his imperial master during this second visit in a degree which excited surprise at the time; the intercourse with Charles at this tragic moment of his career, when, sick and disappointed, he aspired only to the consolations of faith, seeing his sovereign remedy in the soothing balm of utter peace, may have worked to deepen the gloom which was overspreading the painter's art if not his soul. It is not to be believed, all the same, that this atmosphere of unrest and misgiving, of faith coloured by an element of terror, in itself operated so strongly as unaided to give a final form to Titian's sacred works. There was in this respect kinship of spirit between the mighty ruler and his servant; Titian's art had already become sadder and more solemn, had already shown a more sombre passion. The tragic gloom is now to become more and more intense, until we come to the climax in the astonishing *Pietà* left unfinished when the end comes a quarter of a century later still.

And with this change in the whole atmosphere of the sacred art comes another in the inverse sense, which, being an essential trait, must be described, though to do so is not quite easy. Titian becomes more and more merely sensuous in his conception of the beauty of women. He betrays in his loss of serenity that he is less than heretofore impervious to the stings of an invading sensuality, which serves to make of his mythological and erotic scenes belonging to this late time a tribute to the glories of the flesh unennobled by the gilding touch of the purer flame. And the painter who, when Charles V. retired into his solitude, had suffered the feeble flame of his life to die slowly out, was to go on working for King Philip, as fierce in the intensity of his physical passion as in the fervour of his faith, would receive encouragement to develop to the full these seemingly conflicting tendencies of sacred and amorous passion.

The Spanish prince whom it was the master's most important task on this occasion to portray was then but twenty-four years of age, and youth served not indeed to hide, but in a slight measure to attenuate, some of his most characteristic physical defects. His unattractive person even then, however, showed some of the most repellent peculiarities of his father and his race. He had the supreme distinction of Charles but not his majesty, more than his haughty reserve, even less than his power of enlisting sympathy. In this most difficult of tasks – the portrayal that should be at one and the same time true in its essence, distinguished, and as sympathetic as might be under the circumstances, of so unlovable a personage – Titian won a new victory. His *Prince Philip of Austria in Armour* at the Prado is one of his most complete and satisfying achievements, from every point of view. A veritable triumph of art, but as usual a triumph to which the master himself disdains to call attention, is the rendering of the damascened armour, the puffed hose, and the white silk stockings and shoes.

The two most important variations executed by the master, or under his immediate direction, are the full-lengths of the Pitti Palace and the Naples Museum, in both of which sumptuous court-dress replaces the gala military costume. They are practically identical, both in the design and the working out, save that in the Florence example Philip stands on a grass plot in front of a colonnade, while in that of Naples the background is featureless. As the pictures are now seen, that in the Pitti is marked by greater subtlety in the characterisation of the head, while the Naples canvas appears the more brilliant as regards the working out of the costume and accessories.

To the period of Titian's return from the second visit to Augsburg belongs a very remarkable portrait which of late years there has been some disinclination to admit as his own work. This is the imposing full-length portrait which stands forth as the crowning decoration of the beautiful and well-ordered gallery at Cassel. In the days when it was sought to obtain *quand même* a striking designation for a great picture, it was christened *Alfonso d'Avalos, Marqués del Vasto*. More recently, with some greater show of probability, it has been called *Guidobaldo II., Duke of Urbino*. In the *Jahrbuch der königlich-preussischen Kunstsammlungen*,[*43] Herr Carl Justi, ever bold and ingenious in hypothesis, strives, with the support of a mass of corroborative evidence that cannot be here quoted, to prove that the splendid personage presented is a Neapolitan nobleman of the highest rank, Giovan Francesco Acquaviva, Duke of Atri. There is the more reason to accept his conjecture since it helps us to cope with certain difficulties presented by the picture itself. It may be conceded at the outset that there are disturbing elements in it, well calculated to give pause to the student of Titian. The handsome patrician, a little too proud of his rank, his magnificent garments and accoutrements, his virile beauty, stands fronting the spectator in a dress of crimson and gold, wearing a plumed and jewelled hat, which in its elaboration closely borders on the grotesque, and holding a hunting-spear. Still more astonishing in its exaggeration of a

Venetian mode in portraiture[*44] is the great crimson, dragon-crowned helmet which, on the left of the canvas, Cupid himself supports. To the right, a rival even of Love in the affections of our enigmatical personage, a noble hound rubs himself affectionately against the stalwart legs of his master. Far back stretches a prospect singularly unlike those rich-toned studies of sub-Alpine regions in which Titian as a rule revels. It has an august but more colourless beauty recalling the middle Apennines; one might almost say that it prefigures those prospects of inhospitable Sierra which, with their light, delicate tonality, so admirably relieve and support the portraits of Velazquez. All this is unusual, and still more so is the want of that aristocratic gravity, of that subordination of mere outward splendour to inborn dignity, which mark Titian's greatest portraits throughout his career. The splendid materials for the picture are not as absolutely digested, as absolutely welded into one consistent and harmonious whole, as with such authorship one would expect. But then, on the other hand, take the magnificent execution in the most important passages: the distinguished silvery tone obtained notwithstanding the complete red-and-gold costume and the portentous crimson helmet; the masterly brush-work in these last particulars, in the handsome virile head of the model and the delicate flesh of the *amorino*. The dog might without exaggeration be pronounced the best, the truest in movement, to be found in Venetian art – indeed, in art generally, until Velazquez appears. Herr Carl Justi's happy conjecture helps us, if we accept it, to get over some of these difficulties and seeming contradictions. The Duke of Atri belonged to a great Neapolitan family, exiled and living at the French court under royal countenance and protection. The portrait was painted to be sent back to France, to which, indeed, its whole subsequent history belongs. Under such circumstances the young nobleman would naturally desire to affirm his rank and pretensions as emphatically as might be; to outdo in splendour and *prestance* all previous sitters to Titian; to record himself apt in war, in the chase, in love, and more choice in the fashion of his appointments than any of his compeers in France or Italy.

An importance to which it is surely not entitled in the life-work of the master is given to the portrait of the Legate Beccadelli, executed in the month of July 1552, and included among the real and fancied masterpieces of the Tribuna in the Uffizi. To the writer it has always appeared the most nearly tiresome and perfunctory of Titian's more important works belonging to the same class. Perhaps the elaborate legend inscribed on the paper held by the prelate, including the unusual form of signature "Titianus Vecellius faciebat Venetiis MDLII, mense Julii," may have been the cause that the canvas has attracted an undue share of attention.[*45] At p. 218 of Crowe and Cavalcaselle's second volume we get, under date the 11th of October 1552, Titian's first letter to Philip of Spain. There is mention in it of a *Queen of Persia*, which the artist does not expressly declare to be his own work, and of a *Landscape* and *St. Margaret* previously sent by Ambassador Vargas ("… il Paesaggio et il ritratto di Sta. Margarita mandatovi per avanti"). The comment of the biographers on this is that "for the first time in the annals of Italian painting we hear of a picture which claims to be nothing more than a landscape, etc." Remembering, however, that when in 1574, at the end of his life, our master sent in to Philip's secretary, Antonio Perez, a list of paintings delivered from time to time, but not paid for, he described the *Venere del Pardo*, or *Jupiter and Antiope*, as "La nuda con il paese con el satiro," would it not be fair to assume that the description *Il Paesaggio et il ritratto di Sta. Margarita* means one and the same canvas – *The Figure of St. Margaret in a Landscape*? Thus should we be relieved from the duty of searching among the authentic works of the master of Cadore for a landscape pure and simple, and in the process stumbling across a number of spurious and doubtful things. The *St. Margaret* is evidently the picture which, having been many years at the Escorial, now hangs in the Prado Gallery. Obscured and darkened though it is by the irreparable outrages of time, it may be taken as a very characteristic example of Titian's late but not latest manner in

❖ 98

sacred art. In the most striking fashion does it exhibit that peculiar gloom and agitation of the artist face to face with religious subjects which at an earlier period would have left his serenity undisturbed. The saint, uncertain of her triumph, armed though she is with the Cross, flees in affright from the monster whose huge bulk looms, terrible even in overthrow, in the darkness of the foreground. To the impression of terror communicated by the whole conception the distance of the lurid landscape – a city in flames – contributes much.

In the spring and summer of 1554 were finished for Philip of Spain the *Danaë* of Madrid; for Mary, Queen of Hungary, a *Madonna Addolorata*; for Charles V. the *Trinity*, to which he had with Titian devoted so much anxious thought. The *Danaë* of the Prado, less grandiose, less careful in finish than the Naples picture, is painted with greater spontaneity and *élan* than its predecessor, and vibrates with an undisguisedly fleshly passion. Is it to the taste of Philip or to a momentary touch of cynicism in Titian himself that we owe the deliberate dragging down of the conception until it becomes symbolical of the lowest and most venal form of love? In the Naples version Amor, a fairly-fashioned divinity of more or less classic aspect, presides; in the Madrid and subsequent interpretations of the legend, a grasping hag, the attendant of Danaë, holds out a cloth, eager to catch her share of the golden rain. In the St. Petersburg version, which cannot be accounted more than an atelier piece, there is, with some slight yet appreciable variations, a substantial agreement with the Madrid picture. Of this Hermitage *Danaë* there is a replica in the collection of the Duke of Wellington at Apsley House. In yet another version (also a contemporary atelier piece), which is in the Imperial Gallery at Vienna, and has for that reason acquired a certain celebrity, the greedy duenna is depicted in full face, and holds aloft a chased metal dish.

Satisfaction of a very different kind was afforded to Queen Mary of Hungary and Charles V. The lady obtained a *Christ appearing to the Magdalen*, which was for a long time preserved at the Escorial, where there is still to be found a bad copy of it. A mere fragment of the original, showing a head and bust of Christ holding a hoe in his left hand, has been preserved, and is now No. 489 in the gallery of the Prado. Even this does not convince the student that Titian's own brush had a predominant share in the performance. The letter to Charles V., dated from Venice the 10th of September 1554, records the sending of a *Madonna Addolorata* and the great *Trinity*. These, together with another *Virgen de los Dolores* ostensibly by Titian, and the *Ecce Homo* already mentioned, formed afterwards part of the small collection of devotional paintings taken by Charles to his monastic retreat at Yuste, and appropriated after his death by Philip. If the picture styled *La Dolorosa*, and now No. 468 in the gallery of the Prado, is indeed the one painted for the great monarch who was so sick in body and spirit, so fast declining to his end, the suspicion is aroused that the courtly Venetian must have acted with something less than fairness towards his great patron, since the *Addolorata* cannot be acknowledged as his own work. Still less can we accept as his own that other *Virgen de los Dolores*, now No. 475 in the same gallery.

It is very different with the *Trinity*, called in Spain *La Gloria*, and now No. 462 in the same gallery. Though the master must have been hampered by the express command that the Emperor should be portrayed as newly arisen from the grave and adoring the *Trinity* in an agony of prayer, and with him the deceased Empress Isabel, Queen Mary of Hungary, and Prince Philip, also as suppliants, he succeeded in bringing forth not indeed a complete masterpiece, but a picture all aspiration and fervent prayer – just the work to satisfy the yearnings of the man who, once the mightiest, was then the loneliest and saddest of mortals on earth. The crown and climax of the whole is the group of the Trinity itself, awful in majesty, dazzling in the golden radiance of its environment, and, beautifully linking it with mortality, the blue-robed figure of the Virgin, who stands on a lower eminence of cloud as she intercedes for the human race, towards whom her pitying gaze is directed. It would be absurd to pretend that we have here a work entitled, in virtue of the perfect achievement of all that has been sought for, to rank with such earlier masterpieces as the *Assunta* or the *St. Peter Martyr*. Yet it represents in one way sacred art of a higher, a more inspired order, and contains some pictorial beauties – such as the great central group – of which Titian would not in those earlier days have been equally capable.

There is another descent, though not so marked a one as in the case of the *Danaë*, with the *Venus and Adonis* painted for Philip, the new King-Consort of England, and forwarded by the artist to London in the autumn of 1554. That the picture now in the *Sala de la Reina Isabel* at Madrid is this original is proved, in the first place, by the quality of the flesh-painting, the silvery shimmer, the vibration of the whole, the subordination of local colour to general tone, yet by no means to the point of extinction – all these being distinctive qualities of this late time. It is further proved by the fact that it still shows traces of the injury of which Philip complained when he received the picture in London. A long horizontal furrow is clearly to be seen running right across the canvas. Apart from the consideration that pupils no doubt had a hand in the work, it lacks, with all its decorative elegance and felicity of movement, the charm with which Titian, both much earlier in his career and later on towards the end, could invest such mythological subjects.[*46] That the aim of the artist was not a very high one, or this *poesia* very near to his heart, is demonstrated by the amusingly material fashion in which he recommends it to his royal patron. He says that "if in the *Danaë* the forms were to be seen front-wise, here was occasion to look at them from a contrary direction – a pleasant variety for the ornament of a *Camerino*." Our worldly-wise painter evidently knew that material allurements as well as supreme art were necessary to captivate Philip. It cannot be alleged, all the same, that this purely sensuous mode of conception was not perfectly in consonance with his own temperament, with his own point of view, at this particular stage in his life and practice.

The new Doge Francesco Venier had, upon his accession in 1554, called upon Titian to paint, besides his own portrait, the orthodox votive picture of his predecessor Marcantonio Trevisan, and this official performance was duly completed in January 1555, and hung in the Sala de' Pregadi. At the same time Venier determined that thus tardily the memory of a long – deceased Doge, Antonio Grimani, should be rehabilitated by the dedication to him of a similar but more dramatic and allusive composition. The commission for this piece also was given to Titian, who made good progress with it, yet for reasons unexplained never carried the important undertaking to completion. It remained in the workshop at the time of his death, and was completed – with what divergence from the original design we cannot authoritatively say – by assistants. Antonio Grimani, supported by members of his house, or officers attached to his person, kneels in adoration before an emblematic figure of Faith which appears in the clouds holding the cross and chalice, which winged child-angels help to support, and haloed round with an oval glory of cherubim – a conception, by the way, quite new and not at all orthodox. To the left appears a majestic figure of St. Mark, while the clouds upon which Faith is upborne, rise just sufficiently to show a very realistic prospect of Venice. There is not to be found in the whole life-work of Titian a clumsier or more disjointed composition as a whole, even making the necessary allowances for alterations, additions, and restorations. Though the figure of Faith is a sufficiently noble conception in itself, the group which it makes with the attendant angels is inexplicably heavy and awkward in arrangement; the flying *pulli* have none of the audacious grace and buoyancy that Lotto or Correggio would have imparted to them, none of the rush of Tintoretto. The noble figure of St. Mark must be of Titian's designing, but is certainly not of his painting, while the corresponding figure on the other side is neither the one nor the other. Some consolation is afforded by the figure of the kneeling Doge himself, which is a masterpiece – not less in the happy expression of naïve adoration than in the rendering, with

matchless breadth and certainty of brush, of burnished armour in
which is mirrored the glow of the Doge's magnificent state robes.

CHAPTER IV

It was in the month of March 1555 that Titian married his only daughter Lavinia to Cornelio Sarcinelli of Serravalle, thus leaving the pleasant home at Biri Grande without a mistress; for his sister Orsa had been dead since 1549.[*47] It may be convenient to treat here of the various portraits and more or less idealised portrait-pieces in which Titian has immortalised the thoroughly Venetian beauty of his daughter. First we have in the great *Ecce Homo* of Vienna the graceful white-robed figure of a young girl of some fourteen years, placed, with the boy whom she guards, on the steps of Pilate's palace. Then there is the famous piece *Lavinia with a Dish of Fruit*, dating according to Morelli from about 1549, and painted for the master's friend Argentina Pallavicino of Reggio.

This last-named work passed in 1821 from the Solly Collection into the Berlin Gallery. Though its general aspect is splendidly decorative, though it is accounted one of the most popular of all Titian's works, the Berlin picture cannot be allowed to take the highest rank among his performances of the same class. Its fascinations are of the obvious and rather superficial kind, its execution is not equal in vigour, freedom, and accent to the best that the master did about the same time. It is pretty obvious here that only the head is adapted from that of Lavinia, the full-blown voluptuous form not being that of the youthful maiden, who could not moreover have worn this sumptuous and fanciful costume except in the studio. In the strongest contrast to the conscious allurement of this showpiece is the demure simplicity of mien in the avowed portrait *Lavinia as a Bride* in the Dresden Gallery. In this last she wears a costume of warm white satin and a splendid necklace and earrings of pearls. Morelli has pointed out that the fan, in the form of a little flag which she holds, was only used in Venice by newly betrothed ladies; and this fixes the time of the portrait as 1555, the date of the marriage contract. The execution is beyond all comparison finer here, the colour more transparent in its warmth, than in the more celebrated Berlin piece. Quite eight or ten years later than this must date the *Salome* of the Prado Gallery, which is in general design a variation of the *Lavinia* of Berlin. The figure holding up – a grim substitute for the salver of fruit – the head of St. John on a charger has probably been painted without any fresh reference to the model. The writer is unable to agree with Crowe and Cavalcaselle when they affirm that this *Salome* is certainly painted by one of the master's followers. The touch is assuredly Titian's own in the very late time, and the canvas, though much slighter and less deliberate in execution than its predecessors, is in some respects more spontaneous, more vibrant in touch. Second to none as a work of art – indeed more striking than any in the naïve and fearless truth of the rendering – is the *Lavinia Sarcinelli as a Matron* in the Dresden Gallery. Morelli surely exaggerates a little when he describes Lavinia here as a woman of forty. Though the demure, bright-eyed maiden has grown into a self-possessed Venetian dame of portentous dimensions, Sarcinelli's spouse is fresh still, and cannot be more than two-or three-and-thirty. This assumption, if accepted, would fix the time of origin of the picture at about 1565, and, reasoning from analogies of technique, this appears to be a more acceptable date than the year 1570-72, at which Morelli would place it.

One of the most important chapters in our master's life closed with the death of Aretino, which took place suddenly on the 21st of October 1556. He had been sitting at table with friends far into the night or morning. One of them, describing to him a farcical incident of Rabelaisian quality, he threw himself back in his chair in a fit of laughter, and slipping on the polished floor, was thrown with great force on his head and killed almost instantaneously. This was indeed the violent and sudden death of the strong, licentious man; poetic justice could have devised no more fitting end to such a life.

In the year 1558 Crowe and Cavalcaselle, for very sufficient reasons, place the *Martyrdom of St. Lawrence*, now preserved in the hideously over-ornate Church of the Jesuits at Venice. To the very remarkable analysis which they furnish of this work, the writer feels unable to add anything appreciable by way of comment, for the simple reason that though he has seen it many times, on no occasion has he been fortunate enough to obtain such a light as would enable him to judge the picture on its own merits as it now stands.[*48] Of a design more studied in its rhythm, more akin to the Florentine and Roman schools, than anything that has appeared since the *St. Peter Martyr*, with a *mise-en-scène* more classical than anything else from Titian's hand that can be pointed to, the picture may be guessed, rather than seen, to be also a curious and subtle study of conflicting lights. On the one hand we have that of the gruesome martyrdom itself, and of a huge torch fastened to the carved shaft of a pedestal; on the other, that of an effulgence from the skies, celestial in brightness, shedding its consoling beams on the victim.

The *Christ crowned with Thorns*, which long adorned the church of S. Maria delle Grazie at Milan, and is now in the Long Gallery of the Louvre, may belong to about this time, but is painted with a larger and more generous brush, with a more spontaneous energy, than the carefully studied piece at the Gesuiti. The tawny harmonies finely express in their calculated absence of freshness the scene of brutal and unholy violence so dramatically enacted before our eyes. The rendering of muscle, supple and strong under the living epidermis, the glow of the flesh, the dramatic momentariness of the whole, have not been surpassed even by Titian. Of the true elevation, of the spiritual dignity that the subject calls for, there is, however, little or nothing. The finely limbed Christ is as coarse in type and as violent in action as his executioners; sublimity is reached, strange to say, only in the bust of Tiberius, which crowns the rude archway through which the figures have issued into the open space. Titian is here the precursor of the *Naturalisti* – of Caravaggio and his school. Yet, all the same, how immeasurable is the distance between the two!

On the 21st of September 1558 died the imperial recluse of Yuste, once Charles V., and it is said his last looks were steadfastly directed towards that great canvas *The Trinity*, which to devise with Titian had been one of his greatest consolations at a moment when already earthly glories held him no more. Philip, on the news of his father's death, retired for some weeks to the monastery of Groenendale, and thence sent a despatch to the Governor of Milan, directing payment of all the arrears of the pensions "granted to Titian by Charles his father (now in glory)," adding by way of unusual favour a postscript in his own hand.[*49] Orazio Vecellio, despatched by his father in the spring of 1559 to Milan to receive the arrears of pension, accepted the hospitality of the sculptor Leone Leoni, who was then living in splendid style in a palace which he had built and adorned for himself in the Lombard city. He was the rival in art as well as the mortal enemy of Benvenuto Cellini, and as great a ruffian as he, though one less picturesque in blackguardism. One day early in June, when Orazio, having left Leoni's house, had returned to superintend the removal of certain property, he was set upon, and murderously assaulted by the perfidious host and his servants. The whole affair is wrapped in obscurity. It remains uncertain whether vengeance, or hunger after the arrears of Titian's pension, or both, were the motives which incited Leoni to attempt the crime. Titian's passionate reclamations, addressed immediately to Philip II., met with but partial success, since the sculptor, himself a great favourite with the court of Spain, was punished only with fine and banishment, and the affair was afterwards compromised by the payment of a sum of money.

Titian's letter of September 22, 1559, to Philip II. announces the despatch of the companion pieces *Diana and Calisto* and *Diana and Actæon*, as well as of an *Entombment* intended to replace a painting of the same subject which had been lost on the way. The two celebrated canvases,[*50] now in the Bridgewater Gallery, are so familiar that they need no new description. Judging by the repetitions, reductions, and copies that exist in the Imperial Gallery of Vienna, the Prado Gallery, the Yarborough Collection, and elsewhere, these mythological *poesie* have captivated the world far more than the fresher and lovelier painted poems of the earlier time – the *Worship of Venus*, the *Bacchanal,* the *Bacchus and Ariadne.* At no previous period has Titian wielded the brush with greater *maestria* and ease than here, or united a richer or more transparent glow with greater dignity of colour. About the compositions themselves, if we are to take them as the *poesie* that Titian loved to call them, there is a certain want of significance, neither the divine nor the human note being struck with any depth or intensity of vibration. The glamour, the mystery, the intimate charm of the early pieces is lost, and there is felt, enwrapping the whole, that sultry atmosphere of untempered sensuousness which has already, upon more than one occasion, been commented upon. That this should be so is only natural when creative power is not extinguished by old age, but is on the contrary coloured with its passion, so different in quality from that of youth.

The *Entombment*, which went to Madrid with the mythological pieces just now discussed, serves to show how vivid was Titian's imagination at this point, when he touched upon a sacred theme, and how little dependent he was in this field on the conceptions of his earlier prime. A more living passion informs the scene, a more intimate sympathy colours it, than we find in the noble *Entombment* of the Louvre, much as the picture which preceded it by so many years excels the Madrid example in fineness of balance, in dignity, in splendour and charm of colour. Here the personages are set free by the master from all academic trammels, and express themselves with a greater spontaneity in grief. The colour, too, of which the general scheme is far less attractive to the eye than in the Louvre picture, blazes forth in one note of lurid splendour in the red robe of the saint who supports the feet of the dead Christ.

In this same year Titian painted on the ceiling of the ante-chamber to Sansovino's great Library in the Piazzetta the allegorical figure *Wisdom*, thus entering into direct competition with young Paolo Veronese, Schiavone, and the other painters who, striving in friendly rivalry, had been engaged a short time before on the ceiling of the great hall in the same building. This noble design contains a pronounced reminiscence of Raphael's incomparable allegorical figures in the Camera della Segnatura, but excels them as much in decorative splendour and facile breadth of execution as it falls behind them in sublimity of inspiration.

Crowe and Cavalcaselle are probably right in assigning the great *Cornaro Family* in the collection of the Duke of Northumberland to the year 1560 or thereabouts. Little seen of late years, and like most Venetian pictures of the sixteenth century shorn of some of its glory by time and the restorer, this family picture appears to the writer to rank among Titian's masterpieces in the domain of portraiture, and to be indeed the finest portrait-group of this special type that Venice has produced. In the simplicity and fervour of the conception Titian rises to heights which he did not reach in the *Madonna di Casa Pesaro*, where he is hampered by the necessity for combining a votive picture with a series of avowed portraits. It is pretty clear that this *Cornaro* picture, like the Pesaro altar-piece, must have been commissioned to commemorate a victory or important political event in the annals of the illustrious family. Search among their archives and papers, if they still exist, might throw light upon this point, and fix more accurately the date of the magnificent work. In the open air – it may be outside some great Venetian church – an altar has been erected, and upon it is placed a crucifix, on either side of which are church candles, blown this way and the other by the wind. Three generations of patricians kneel in prayer and thanksgiving, taking precedence according to age, six handsome boys, arranged in groups of three on either side of the canvas, furnishing an element of great pictorial attractiveness but no vital significance. The act of worship acquires here more reality and a profounder meaning than it can have in those vast altar-pieces in which the divine favour is symbolised by the actual presence of the Madonna and Child. An open-air effect has been deliberately aimed at and attained, the splendid series of portraits being relieved against the cloud-flecked blue sky with a less sculptural plasticity than the master would have given to them in an indoor scheme. This is another admirable example of the dignity and reserve which Titian combines with sumptuous colour at this stage of his practice. His mastery is not less but greater, subtler, than that of his more showy and brilliant contemporaries of the younger generation; the result is something that appears as if it must inevitably have been so and not otherwise. The central figure of the patriarch is robed in deep crimson with grayish fur, rather black in shadow; the man in the prime of manhood wears a more positive crimson, trimmed with tawnier fur, browner in shadow; a lighter sheen is on the brocaded mantle of yet another shade of crimson worn by the most youthful of the three patricians. Just the stimulating note to break up a harmony which might otherwise have been of a richness too cloying is furnished – in the master's own peculiar way – by the scarlet stockings of one boy in the right hand group, by the cinnamon sleeve of another.[*51]

To the year 1561 belongs, according to the elaborate inscription on the picture, the magnificent *Portrait of a Man* which is No. 172 in the Dresden Gallery. It presents a Venetian gentleman in his usual habit, but bearing a palm branch such as we associate with saints who have endured martyrdom. Strangely sombre and melancholy in its very reserve is this sensitive face, and the tone of the landscape echoes the pathetic note of disquiet. The canvas bears the signature "Titianus Pictor et Aeques (sic) Caesaris." There group very well with this Dresden picture, though the writer will not venture to assert positively that they belong to exactly the same period, the *St. Dominic* of the Borghese Gallery and the *Knight of Malta* of the Prado Gallery. In all three – in the two secular portraits as in the sacred piece which is also a portrait – the expression given, and doubtless intended, is that of a man who has withdrawn himself in his time of fullest physical vigour from the pomps and vanities of the world, and sadly concentrates his thoughts on matters of higher import.

On the 1st of December 1561 Titian wrote to the king to announce the despatch of a *Magdalen*, which had already been mentioned more than once in the correspondence. According to Vasari and subsequent authorities, Silvio Badoer, a Venetian patrician, saw the masterpiece on the painter's easel, and took it away for a hundred scudi, leaving the master to paint another for Philip. This last has disappeared, while the canvas which remained in Venice cannot be identified with any certainty. The finest extant example of this type of *Magdalen* is undoubtedly that which from Titian's ne'er-do-well son, Pompinio, passed to the Barbarigo family, and ultimately, with the group of Titians forming part of the Barbarigo collection, found its way into the

Imperial Gallery of the Hermitage at St. Petersburg. This answers in every respect to Vasari's eloquent description of the *magna peccatrix*, lovely still in her penitence. It is an embodiment of the favourite subject, infinitely finer and more moving than the much earlier *Magdalen* of the Pitti, in which the artist's sole preoccupation has been the alluring portraiture of exuberant feminine charms. This later *Magdalen*, as Vasari says, "ancorchè che sia bellissima, non muove a lascivia, ma a commiserazione," and the contrary might, without exaggeration, be said of the Pitti picture.[*52] Another of the Barbarigo heirlooms which so passed into the Hermitage is the ever-popular *Venus with the Mirror*, the original of many repetitions and variations. Here, while one winged love holds the mirror, the other proffers a crown of flowers, not to the goddess, but to the fairest of women. The rich mantle of Venetian fashion, the jewels, the coiffure, all show that an idealised portrait of some lovely Cytherean of Venice, and no true mythological piece, has been intended.

At this date, or thereabouts, is very generally placed, with the *Rape of Europa* presently to be discussed, the *Jupiter and Antiope* of the Louvre, more popularly known as the *Venere del Pardo*.[*53] Seeing that the picture is included in the list[*54] sent by Titian to Antonio Perez in 1574, setting forth the titles of canvases delivered during the last twenty-five years, and then still unpaid for, it may well have been completed somewhere about the time at which we have arrived. To the writer it appears nevertheless that it is in essentials the work of an earlier period, taken up and finished thus late in the day for the delectation of the Spanish king. Seeing that the *Venere del Pardo* has gone through two fires – those of the Pardo and the Louvre – besides cleanings, restorations, and repaintings, even more disfiguring, it would be very unsafe to lay undue stress on technique alone. Yet compare the close, sculptural modelling in the figure of Antiope with the broader, looser handling in the figure of Europa; compare the two landscapes, which are even more divergent in style. The glorious sylvan prospect, which adds so much freshness and beauty to the

Venere del Pardo, is conspicuously earlier in manner than, for instance, the backgrounds to the *Diana and Actæon* and *Diana and Calisto* of Bridgewater House. The captivating work is not without its faults, chief among which is the curious awkwardness of design which makes of the composition, cut in two by a central tree, two pictures instead of one. Undeniably, too, there is a certain meanness and triviality in the little nymph or mortal of the foreground, which may, however, be due to the intervention of an assistant. But then, with an elasticity truly astounding in a man of his great age, the master has momentarily regained the poetry of his youthful prime, and with it a measure of that Giorgionesque fragrance which was evaporating already at the close of the early time, when the *Bacchanals* were brought forth. The Antiope herself far transcends in the sovereign charm of her beauty – divine in the truer sense of the word – all Titian's Venuses, save the one in the *Sacred and Profane Love*. The figure comes in some ways nearer even in design, and infinitely nearer in feeling, to Giorgione's *Venus* at Dresden than does the *Venus of Urbino* in the Tribuna, which was closely modelled upon it. And the aged Titian had gone back even a step farther than Giorgione; the group of Antiope with Jupiter in the guise of a Satyr is clearly a reminiscence of a *Nymph surprised by a Satyr* – one of the engravings in the *Hypnerotomachia Poliphili* first published in 1499, but republished with the same illustrations in 1545.[*55]

According to the correspondence published by Crowe and Cavalcaselle there were completed for the Spanish King in April 1562 the *Poesy of Europa carried by the Bull*, and the *Christ praying in the Garden*, while a *Virgin and Child* was announced as in progress.

These paintings, widely divergent as they are in subject, answer very well to each other in technical execution, while in both they differ very materially from the *Venere del Pardo*. The *Rape of Europa*, which has retained very much of its blond brilliancy and charm of colour, affords convincing proof of the unrivalled power with which Titian still wielded the brush at this stage which precedes that of his very last and most impressionistic style. For decorative effect, for "go," for frankness and breadth of execution, it could not be surpassed. Yet hardly elsewhere has the great master approached so near to positive vulgarity as here in the conception of the fair Europa as a strapping wench who, with ample limbs outstretched, complacently allows herself to be carried off by the Bull, making her appeal for succour merely *pour la forme*. What gulfs divide this conception from that of the Antiope, from Titian's earlier renderings of female loveliness, from Giorgione's supreme Venus![*56]

The *Agony in the Garden*, which is still to be found in one of the halls of the Escorial, even now in its faded state serves to evidence the intensity of religious fervour which possessed Titian when, so late in life, he successfully strove to renew the sacred subjects. If the composition – as Crowe and Cavalcaselle assert – does more or less resemble that of the famous *Agony* by Correggio now at Apsley House, nothing could differ more absolutely from the Parmese master's amiable virtuosity than the aged Titian's deep conviction.[*57]

To the year 1562 belongs the nearly profile portrait of the artist, painted by himself with a subtler refinement and a truer revelation of self than is to be found in those earlier canvases of Berlin and the Uffizi in which his late prime still shows as a green and vigorous manhood. This is now in the *Sala de la Reina Isabel* of the Prado. The pale noble head, refined by old age to a solemn beauty, is that of one brought face to face with the world beyond; it is the face of the man who could conceive and paint the sacred pieces of the end, the *Ecce Homo* of Munich and the last *Pietà*, with an awe such as we here read in his eyes. Much less easy is it to connect this likeness with the artist who went on concurrently producing his Venuses, mythological pieces, and pastorals, and joying as much as ever in their production.

Vasari, who, as will be seen, visited Venice in 1566, when he was preparing that new and enlarged edition of the *Lives* which was to appear in 1568, had then an opportunity of renewing his friendly acquaintance with the splendid old man whom he had last seen, already well stricken in years, twenty-one years before in Rome. It must have been at this stage that he formed the judgment as to the latest manner of Titian which is so admirably expressed in his biography of the master. Speaking especially of the *Diana and Actæon,* the *Rape of Europa,* and the *Deliverance of Andromeda,*[*58] he delivers himself as follows: – "It is indeed true that his technical manner in these last is very different from that of his youth. The first works are, be it remembered, carried out with incredible delicacy and pains, so that they can be looked at both at close quarters and from afar. These last ones are done with broad coarse strokes and blots of colour, in such wise that they cannot be appreciated near at hand, but from afar look perfect. This style has been the cause that many, thinking therein to play the imitators and to make a display of practical skill, have produced clumsy, bad pictures. This is so, because, notwithstanding that to many it may seem that Titian's works are done without labour, this is not so in truth, and they who think so deceive themselves. It is, on the contrary, to be perceived that they are painted at many sittings, that they have been worked upon with the colours so many times as to make the labour evident; and this method of execution is judicious, beautiful, astonishing, because it makes the pictures seem living."

No better proof could be given of Vasari's genuine *flair* and intuition as a critic of art than this passage. We seem to hear, not the Tuscan painter bred to regard the style of Michelangelo as an article of faith, to imitate his sculptural smoothness of finish and that of Angelo Bronzino, but some intelligent exponent of impressionistic methods, defending both from attack and from superficial imitation one of the most advanced of modernists.

Among the sacred works produced in this late time is a *Crucifixion,* still preserved in a damaged state in the church of S. Domenico at Ancona. To a period somewhat earlier than that at which we have arrived may belong the late *Madonna and Child in a Landscape* which is No. 1113 in the Alte Pinakothek of Munich.

The writer follows Giovanni Morelli in believing that this is a studio picture touched by the master, and that the splendidly toned evening landscape is all his. He cannot surely be made wholly responsible for the overgrown and inflated figure of the divine *Bambino*, so disproportionate, so entirely wanting in tenderness and charm.

The power of vivid conception, the spontaneous fervour which mark Titian's latest efforts in the domain of sacred art, are very evident in the great *St. Jerome* of the Brera here reproduced. Cima, Basaiti, and most of the Bellinesques had shown an especial affection for the subject, and it had been treated too by Lotto, by Giorgione, by Titian himself; but this is surely as noble and fervent a rendering as Venetian art in its prime has brought forth. Of extraordinary majesty and beauty is the landscape, with its mighty trees growing out of the abrupt mountain slope, close to the naked rock.

In the autumn of 1564 we actually find the venerable master, then about eighty-seven years of age, taking a journey to Brescia in connection with an important commission given to him for the decoration of the great hall in the Palazzo Pubblico at Brescia, to which the Vicentine artist Righetto had supplied the ceiling, and Palladio had added columns and interior wall-decorations. The three great ceiling-pictures, which were afterwards, as a consequence of the contract then entered upon, executed by the master, or rather by his assistants, endured only until 1575, when in the penultimate year of Titian's life they perished in a great fire.

The correspondence shows that the vast *Last Supper* painted for the Refectory of the Escorial, and still to be found there, was finished in October 1564, and that there was much haggling and finessing on the part of the artist before it was despatched to Spain, the object being to secure payment of the arrears of pension still withheld by the Milanese officials. When the huge work did arrive at the Escorial the monks perpetrated upon it one of those acts of vandalism of which Titian was in more than one instance the victim. Finding that the picture would not fit the particular wall of their refectory for which it had been destined, they ruthlessly cut it down, slicing off a large piece of the upper part, and throwing the composition out of balance by the mutilation of the architectural background.

Passing over the *Transfiguration* on the high altar of San Salvatore at Venice, we come to the *Annunciation* in the same church with the signature "Titianus fecit fecit," added by the master, if we are to credit the legend, in indignation that those who commissioned the canvas should have shown themselves dissatisfied even to the point of expressing incredulity as to his share in the performance. Some doubt has been cast upon this story, which may possibly have been evolved on the basis of the peculiar signature. It is at variance with Vasari's statement that Titian held the picture in slight esteem in comparison with his other works. It is not to be contested that for all the fine passages of colour and execution, the general tone is paler in its silveriness, less vibrant and effective on the whole, than in many of the masterpieces which have been mentioned in their turn. But the conception is a novel and magnificent one, contrasting instructively in its weightiness and majesty with the more naïve and pathetic renderings of an earlier time.

The *Education of Cupid,* popularly but erroneously known as *The Three Graces*[*59] is one of the pearls of the Borghese Gallery. It is clearly built in essentials on the master's own *d'Avalos Allegory,* painted many years before. This later allegory shows Venus binding the eyes of Love ere he sallies forth into the world, while his bow and his quiver well-stocked with arrows are brought forward by two of the Graces. In its conception there is no great freshness or buoyancy, no pretence at invention. The aged magician of the brush has interested himself more in the execution than in the imagining of his picture. It is a fine and typical specimen of the painting *di macchia,* which Vasari has praised in a passage already quoted. A work such as this bears in technique much the same relation to the productions of Titian's first period that the great *Family Picture* of Rembrandt at Brunswick does to his work done some thirty-five or forty years before. In both instances it is a life-time of legitimate practice that has permitted the old man to indulge without danger in an abridgment of labour, a synthetic presentment of fact, which means no abatement, but in some ways an enhancement of life, breadth, and pictorial effect. To much about the same time, judging from the handling and the types, belongs the curious allegory, *Religion succoured by Spain* – otherwise *La Fé* – now No. 476 in the gallery of the Prado. This canvas, notwithstanding a marked superficiality of invention as well as of execution, is in essentials the master's own; moreover it can boast its own special decorative qualities, void though it is of any deep significance. The showy figure of Spain holding aloft in one hand a standard, and with the other supporting a shield emblazoned with the arms of the realm, recalls the similar creations of Paolo Veronese. Titian has rarely been less happily inspired than in the figure of Religion, represented as a naked female slave newly released from bondage.

When Vasari in 1566 paid the visit to Venice, of which a word has already been said, he noted, among a good many other things then in progress, the *Martyrdom of St. Lawrence*, based upon that now at the Gesuiti in Venice. This was despatched nearly two years later to the Escorial, where it still occupies its place on the high altar of the mighty church dedicated to St. Lawrence. The Brescian ceiling canvases appeared, too, in his list as unfinished. They were sent to their destination early in 1568, to be utterly destroyed, as has been told, by fire in 1575.

The best proof we have that Titian's artistic power was in many respects at its highest in 1566, is afforded by the magnificent portrait of the Mantuan painter and antiquary Jacopo da Strada, now in the Imperial Gallery at Vienna. It bears, besides the usual late signature of the master, the description of the personage with all his styles and titles, and the date MDLXVI. The execution is again *di macchia*, but magnificent in vitality, as in impressiveness of general effect, swift but not hasty or superficial. The reserve and dignity of former male portraits is exchanged for a more febrile vivacity, akin to that which Lotto had in so many of his finest works displayed. His peculiar style is further recalled in the rather abrupt inclination of the figure and the parallel position of the statuette which it holds. But none other than Titian himself could have painted the superb head, which he himself has hardly surpassed.

It is curious and instructive to find the artist, in a letter addressed to Philip on the 2nd of December 1567, announcing the despatch, together with the just now described altar-piece, *The Martyrdom of St. Lawrence*, of "una pittura d'una Venere ignuda" – the painting of a nude Venus. Thus is the peculiar double current of the aged painter's genius maintained by the demand for both classes of work. He well knows that to the Most Catholic Majesty very secular pieces indeed will be not less acceptable than those much-desired sacred works in which now Titian's power of invention is greatest.

Our master, in his dealings with the Brescians, after the completion of the extensive decorations for the Palazzo Pubblico, was to have proof that Italian citizens were better judges of art than the King of Spain, and more grudging if prompter paymasters. They declared, not without some foundation in fact, that the canvases were not really from the hand of Titian, and refused to pay more than one thousand ducats for them. The negotiation was conducted – as were most others at that time – by the trusty Orazio, who after much show of indignation was compelled at last to accept the proffered payment.

The great victory of Lepanto, gained by the united fleets of Spain and Venice over the Turk on the 7th of October 1571, gave fitting occasion for one of Paolo Veronese's most radiant masterpieces, the celebrated votive picture of the Sala del Collegio, for Tintoretto's *Battle of Lepanto*, but also for one of Titian's feeblest works, the allegory *Philip II. offering to Heaven his Son, the Infant Don Ferdinand*, now No. 470 in the gallery of the

Prado. That Sanchez Coello, under special directions from the king, prepared the sketch which was to serve as the basis for the definitive picture may well have hampered and annoyed the aged master. Still this is but an insufficient excuse for the absurdities of the design, culminating in the figure of the descending angel, who is represented in one of those strained, over-bold attitudes, in which Titian, even at his best, never achieved complete success. That he was not, all the same, a stranger to the work, is proved by some flashes of splendid colour, some fine passages of execution.

In the four pieces now to be shortly described, the very latest and most impressionistic form of Titian's method as a painter is to be observed; all of them are in the highest degree characteristic of this ultimate phase. In the beautiful *Madonna and Child* here reproduced,[*60] the hand, though it no longer works with all trenchant vigour of earlier times, produces a magical effect by means of unerring science and a certainty of touch justifying such economy of mere labour as is by the system of execution suggested to the eye. And then this pathetic motive, the simple realism, the unconventional treatment of which are spiritualised by infinite tenderness, is a new thing in Venetian, nay in Italian art. Precisely similar in execution, and equally restrained in the scheme of colour adopted, is the *Christ crowned with Thorns* of the Alte Pinakothek at Munich, a reproduction with important variations of the better-known picture in the Long Gallery of the Louvre. Less demonstratively and obviously dramatic than its predecessor, the Munich example is, as a realisation of the scene, far truer and more profound in pathos. Nobler beyond compare in His unresisting acceptance of insult and suffering is the Munich Christ than the corresponding figure, so violent in its instinctive recoil from pain, of the Louvre picture.

It is nothing short of startling at the very end of Titian's career to meet with a work which, expressed in this masterly late technique of his, vies in freshness of inspiration with the finest of his early *poesie*. This is the *Nymph and Shepherd*[*61] of the

Imperial Gallery at Vienna, a picture which the world had forgotten until it was added, or rather restored, to the State collection on its transference from the Belvedere to the gorgeous palace which it now occupies. In its almost monochromatic harmony of embrowned silver the canvas embodies more absolutely than any other, save perhaps the final *Pietà*, the ideal of tone-harmony towards which the master in his late time had been steadily tending. Richness and brilliancy of local colour are subordinated, and this time up to the point of effacement, to this luminous monotone, so mysteriously effective in the hands of a master such as Titian. In the solemn twilight which descends from the heavens, just faintly flushed with rose, an amorous shepherd, flower-crowned, pipes to a nude nymph, who, half-won by the appealing strain, turns her head as she lies luxuriously extended on a wild beast's hide, covering the grassy knoll; in the distance a strayed goat browses on the leafage of a projecting branch. It may not be concealed that a note of ardent sensuousness still makes itself felt, as it does in most of the later pieces of the same class. But here, transfigured by a freshness of poetic inspiration hardly to be traced in the master's work in pieces of this order, since those early Giorgionesque days when the sixteenth century was in its youth, it offends no more than does an idyll of Theocritus. Since the *Three Ages* of Bridgewater House, divided from the *Nymph and Shepherd* by nearly seventy years of life and labour, Titian had produced nothing which, apart from the question of technical execution, might so nearly be paralleled with that exquisite pastoral. The early *poesia* gives, wrapped in clear even daylight, the perfect moment of trusting, satisfied love; the late one, with less purity, but, strange to say, with a higher passion, renders, beautified by an evening light more solemn and suggestive, the divine ardours fanned by solitude and opportunity.

And now we come to the *Pietà*,[*62] which so nobly and appropriately closes a career unexampled for duration and sustained achievement. Titian had bargained with the Franciscan monks of the Frari, which contained already the *Assunta* and the *Madonna di Casa Pesaro*, for a grave in the Cappella del Crocifisso, offering in payment a *Pietà*, and this offer had been accepted. But some misunderstanding and consequent quarrel having been the ultimate outcome of the proposed arrangements, he left his great canvas unfinished, and willed that his body should be taken to Cadore, and there buried in the chapel of the Vecelli.

The well-known inscription on the base of the monumental niche which occupies the centre of the *Pietà*, "Quod Titianus inchoatum reliquit, Palma reverenter absolvit, Deoque dicavit opus," records how what Titian had left undone was completed as reverently as might be by Palma Giovine. At this stage – the question being much complicated by subsequent restorations – the effort to draw the line accurately between the work of the master on one hand and that of his able and pious assistant on the other, would be unprofitable. Let us rather strive to appreciate what is left of a creation unique in the life-work of Titian, and in some ways his most sublime invention. Genius alone could have triumphed over the heterogeneous and fantastic surroundings in which he has chosen to enframe his great central group. And yet even these – the great rusticated niche with the gold mosaic of the pelican feeding its young, the statues of Moses on one side and of the Hellespontic Sibyl on the other – but serve to heighten the awe of the spectator. The artificial light is obtained in part from a row of crystal lamps on the cornice of the niche, in part, too, from the torch borne by the beautiful boy-angel who hovers in mid-air, yet another focus of illumination being the body of the dead Christ. This system of lighting furnishes just the luminous half-gloom, the deeply significant chiaroscuro, that the painter requires in order to give the most poignant effect to his last and most thrilling conception of the world's tragedy. As is often the case with Tintoretto, but more seldom with Titian, the eloquent passion breathed forth in this *Pietà* is not to be accounted for by any element or elements of the composition taken separately; it depends to so great an extent on the poetic suggestiveness of the illumination, on the strange and indefinable power of evocation that the aged master here exceptionally commands.

Wonderfully does the terrible figure of the Magdalen contrast in its excess of passion with the sculptural repose, the permanence of the main group. As she starts forward, almost menacing in her grief, her loud and bitter cry seems to ring through space, accusing all mankind of its great crime. It is with a conviction far more intense than has ever possessed him in his prime, with an awe nearly akin to terror, that Titian, himself trembling on the verge of eternity, and painting, too, that which shall purchase his own grave, has produced this profoundly moving work. No more fitting end and crown to the great achievements of the master's old age could well be imagined.

There is no temptation to dwell unnecessarily upon the short period of horror and calamity with which this glorious life came to an end. If Titian had died a year earlier, his biographer might still have wound up with those beautiful words of Vasari's peroration: "E stato Tiziano sanissimo et fortunate quant' alcun altro suo pari sia stato ancor mai; e non ha mai avuto dai cieli se non favori e felicità." Too true it is, alas, that no man's life may be counted happy until its close! Now comes upon the great city this all-enveloping horror of the plague, beginning in 1575, but in 1576 attaining to such vast proportions as to sweep away more than a quarter of the whole population of 190,000 inhabitants. On the 17th of August, 1576, old Titian is attacked and swept away – surprised, as one would like to believe, while still at work on his *Pietà*. Even at such a moment, when panic reigns supreme, and the most honoured, the most dearly beloved are left untended, he is not to be hurried into an unmarked grave. Notwithstanding the sanitary law which forbids the burial of one who has succumbed to the plague in any of the city churches, he receives the supreme and at this awful moment unique honour of solemn obsequies. The body is taken with all due observance to the great church of the Frari, and there interred in the Cappella del Crocifisso, which Titian has already, before the quarrel with the Franciscans, designated as his final resting-place. He is spared the grief of knowing that the favourite son, Orazio, for whom all these years he has laboured and schemed, is to follow him immediately, dying also of the plague, and not even at Biri Grande, but in the Lazzaretto Vecchio, near the Lido; that the incorrigible Pomponio is to succeed and enjoy the inheritance after his own unworthy fashion. He is spared the knowledge of the great calamity of 1577, the destruction by fire of the Sala del Gran Consiglio, and with it, of the *Battle of Cadore*, and most of the noble work done officially for the Doges and the Signoria. One would like to think that this catastrophe of the end must have come suddenly upon the venerable master like a hideous dream, appearing to him, as death often does to those upon whom it descends, less significant than it does to us who read. Instead of remaining fixed in sad contemplation of this short final moment when the radiant orb goes suddenly down below the horizon in storm and cloud, let us keep steadily in view the light as, serene in its far-reaching radiance, it illuminated the world for eighty splendid years. Let us think of Titian as the greatest painter, if not the greatest genius in art, that the world has produced; as, what Vasari with such conviction described him to be, "the man as highly favoured by fortune as any of his kind had ever been before him."[*63]

On the following pages are illustrations of some of the
contemporaries of Titian.

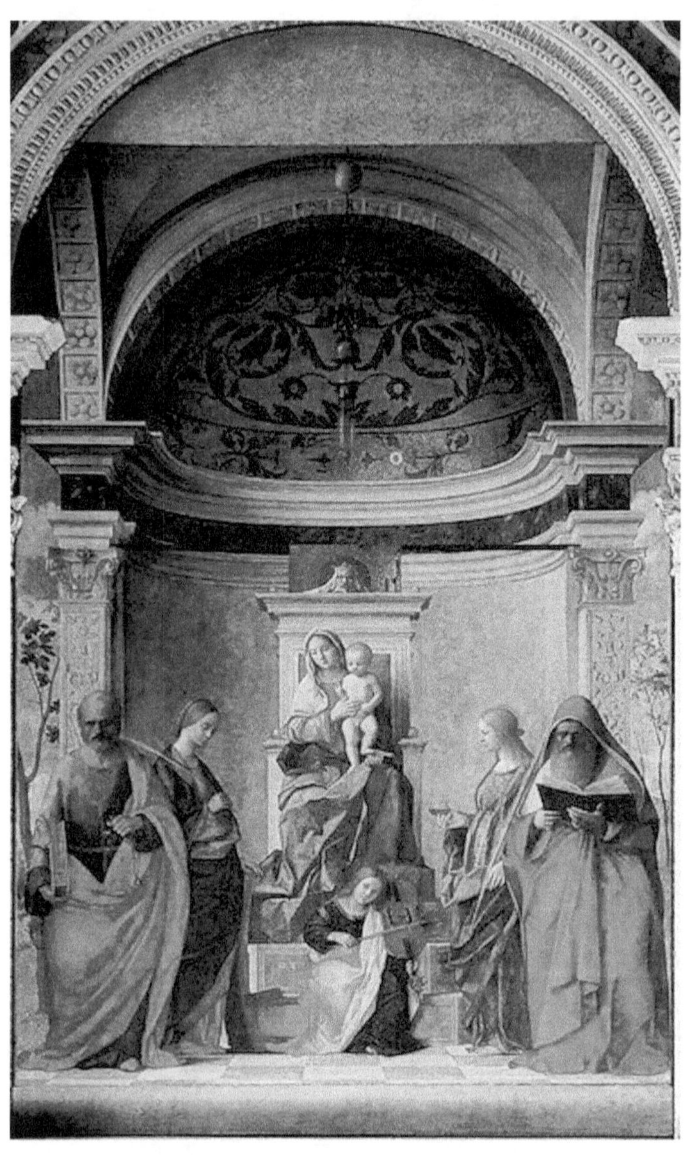

Giovanni Bellini, San Zaccaria Altarpiece

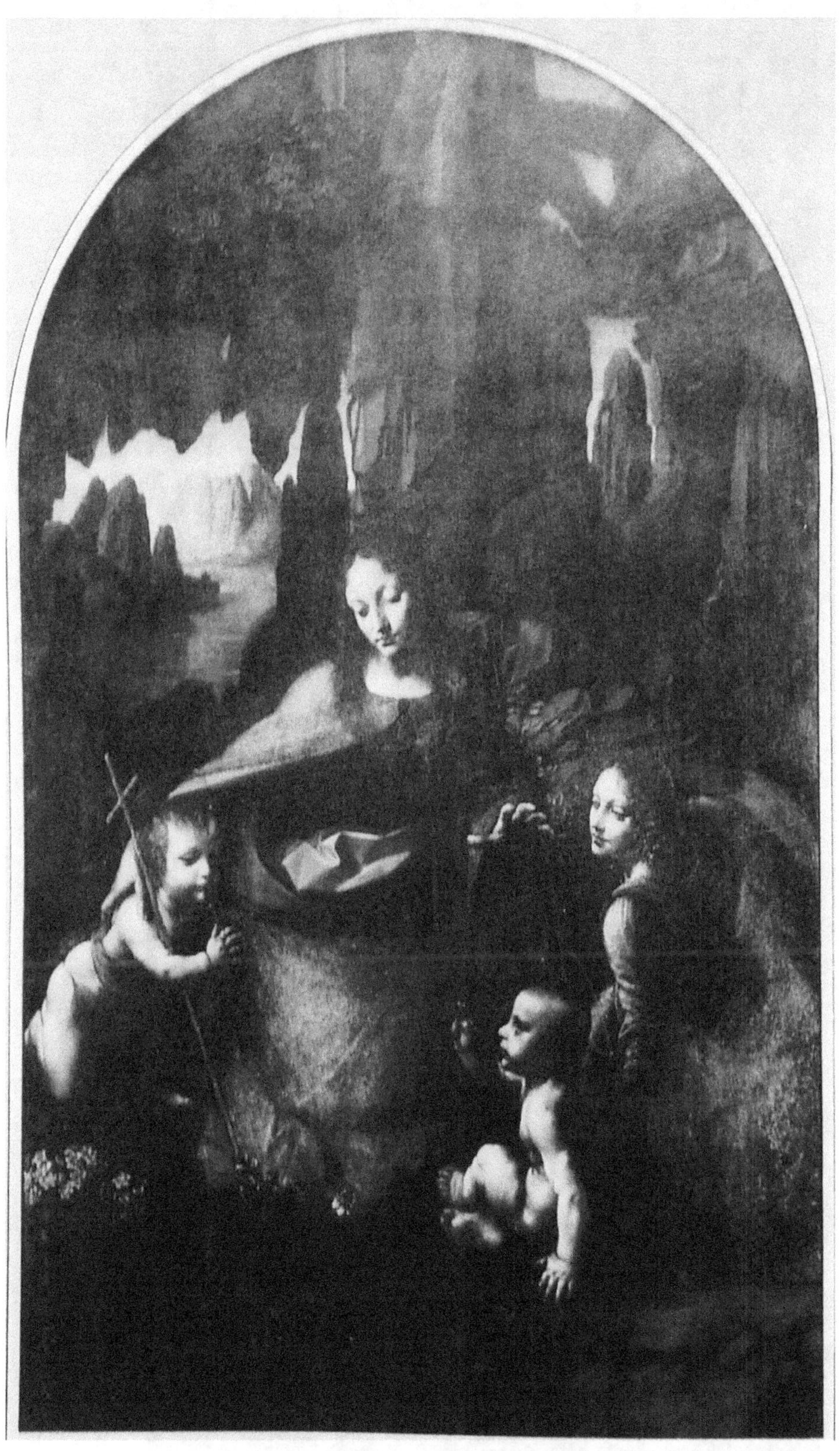

Leonardo da Vinci, *The Virgin of the Rocks*, National Gallery, London

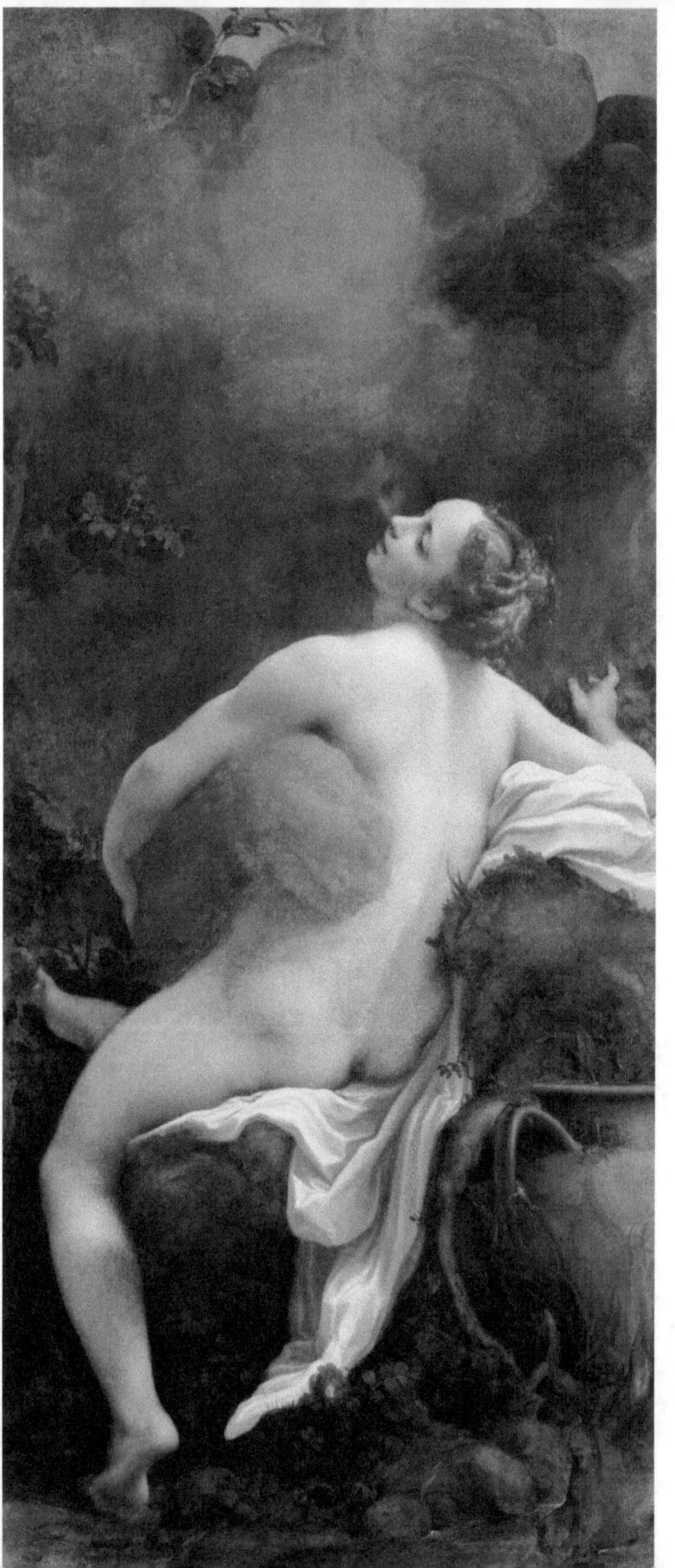

Correggio,
Jupiter and Antiop

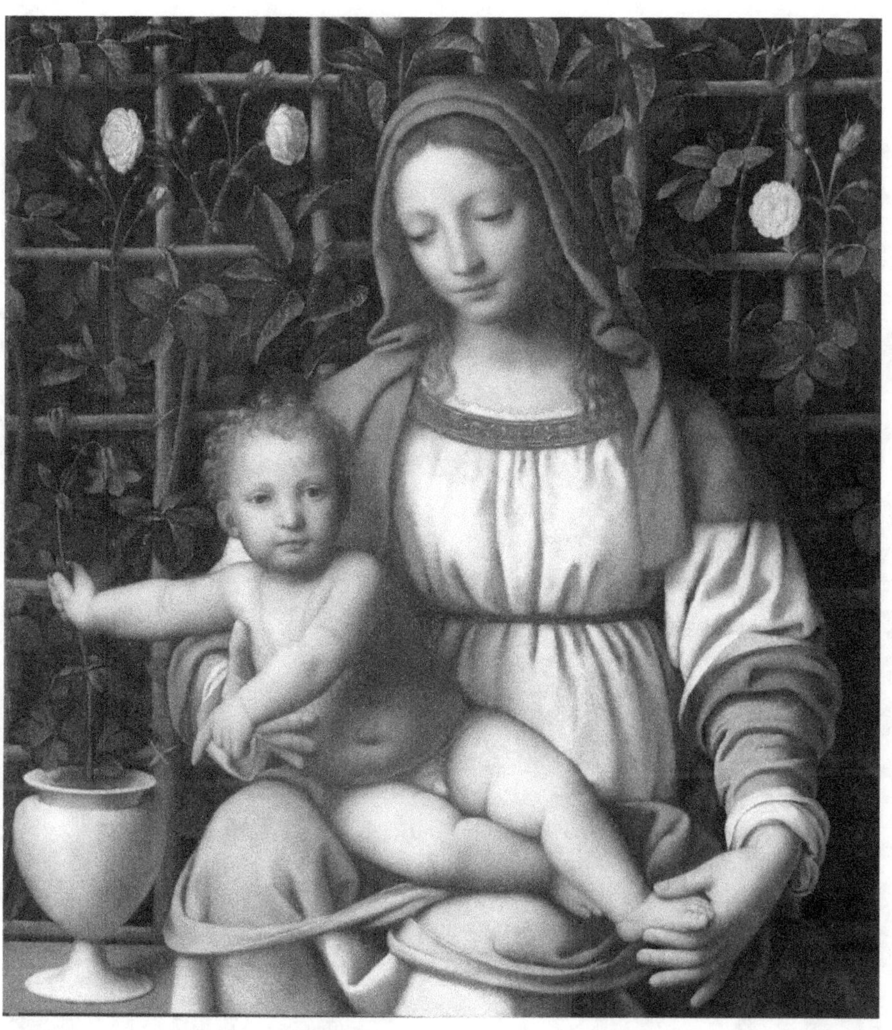

Bernardino Luini, Madonna and Child, Milan

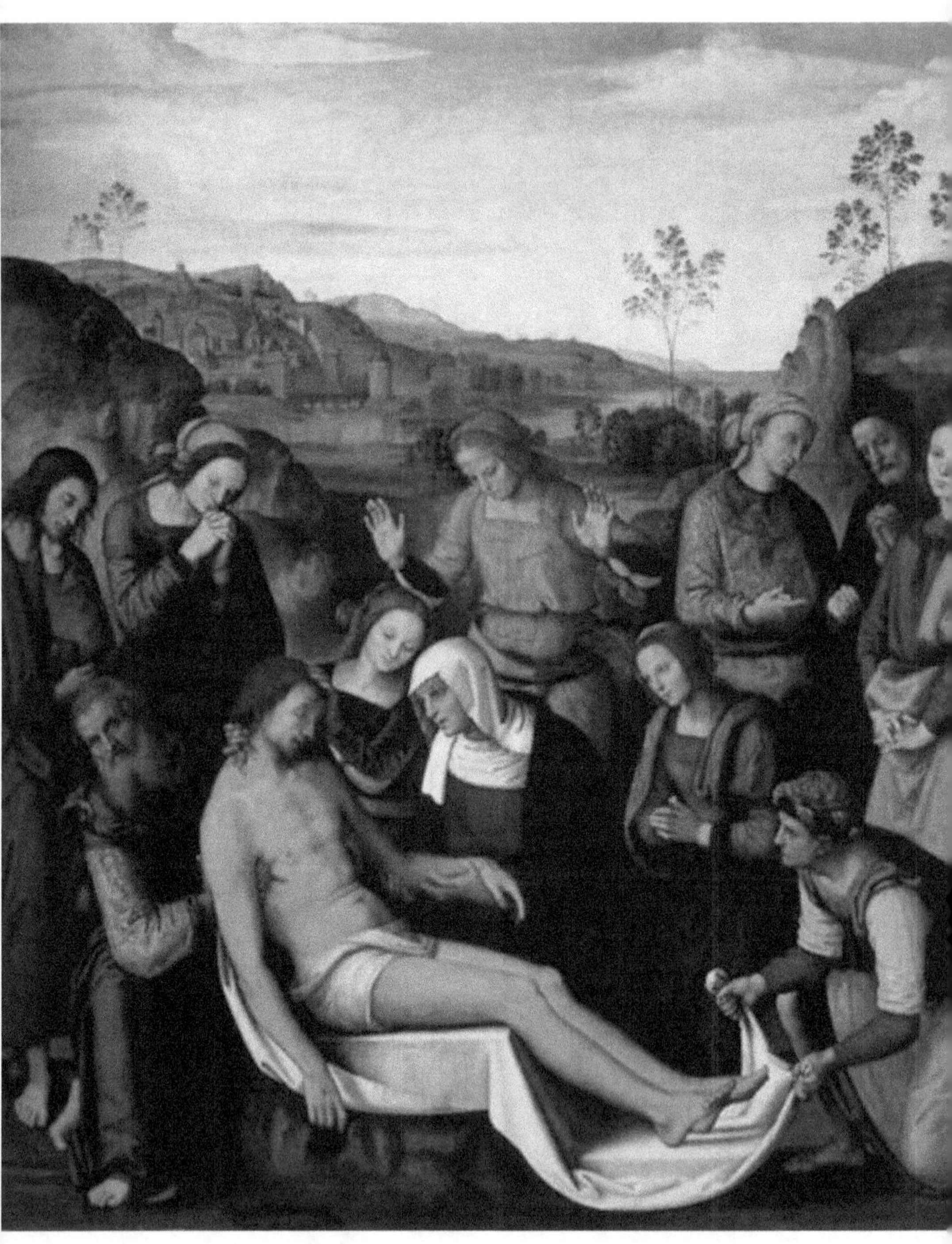

Perugino, The Mourning of the Dead Christ, 1495

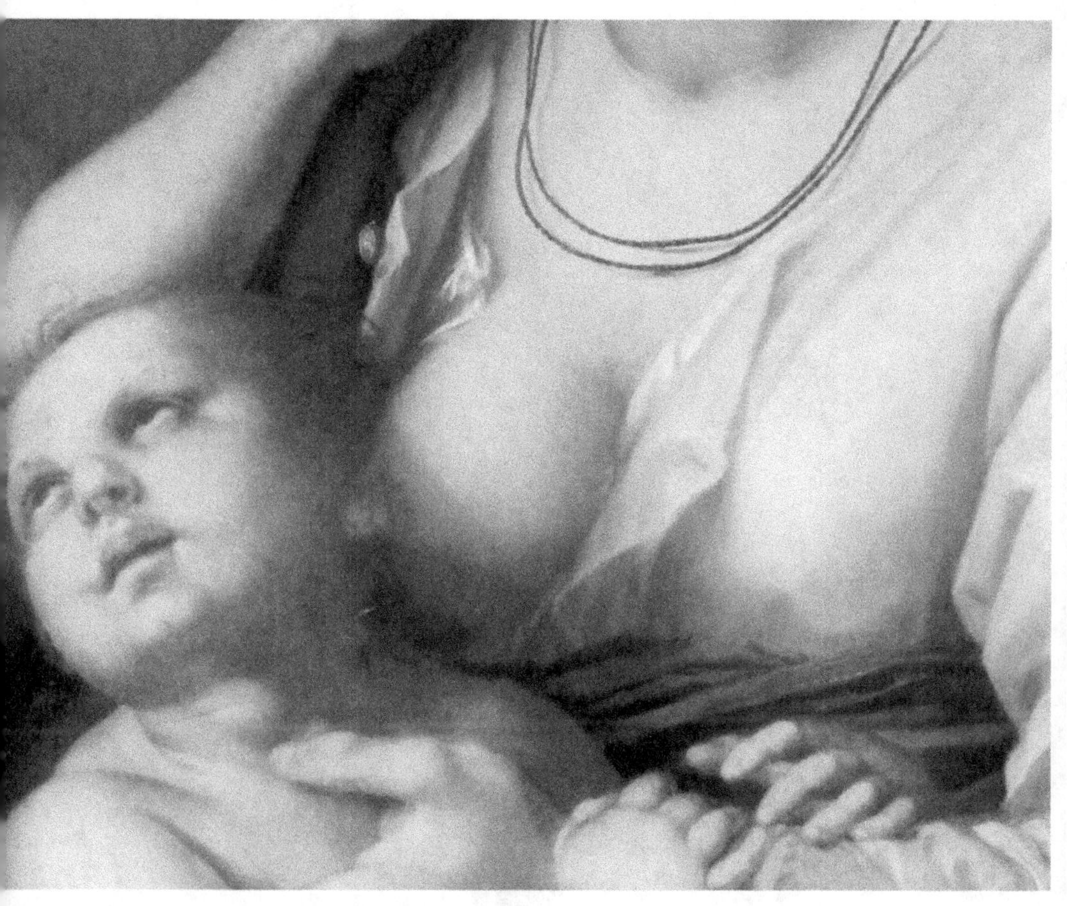

Andrea del Sarto, Madonna and Child, detail

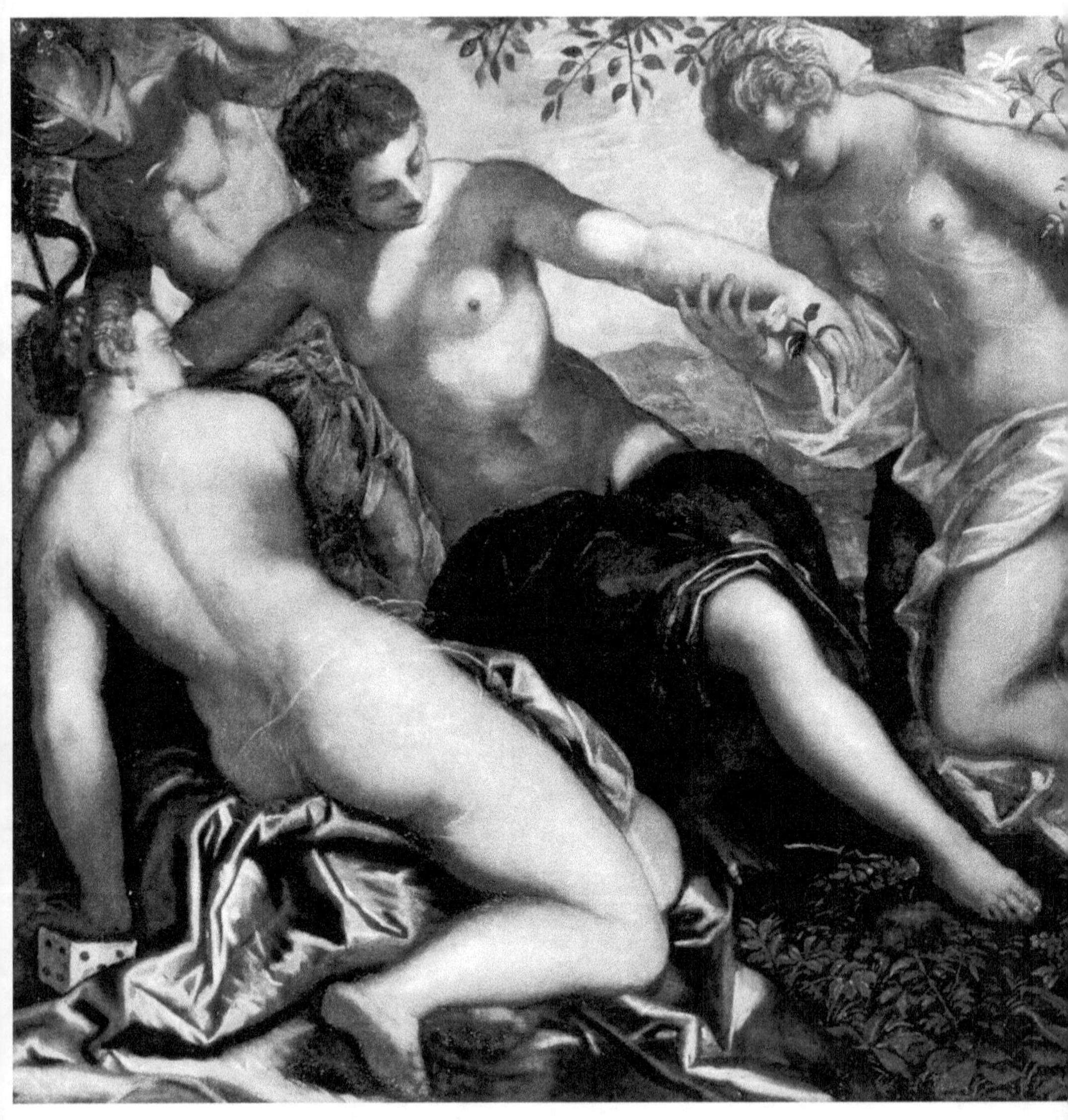

Jacopo Tintoretto, Mercury and the Graces, 1577

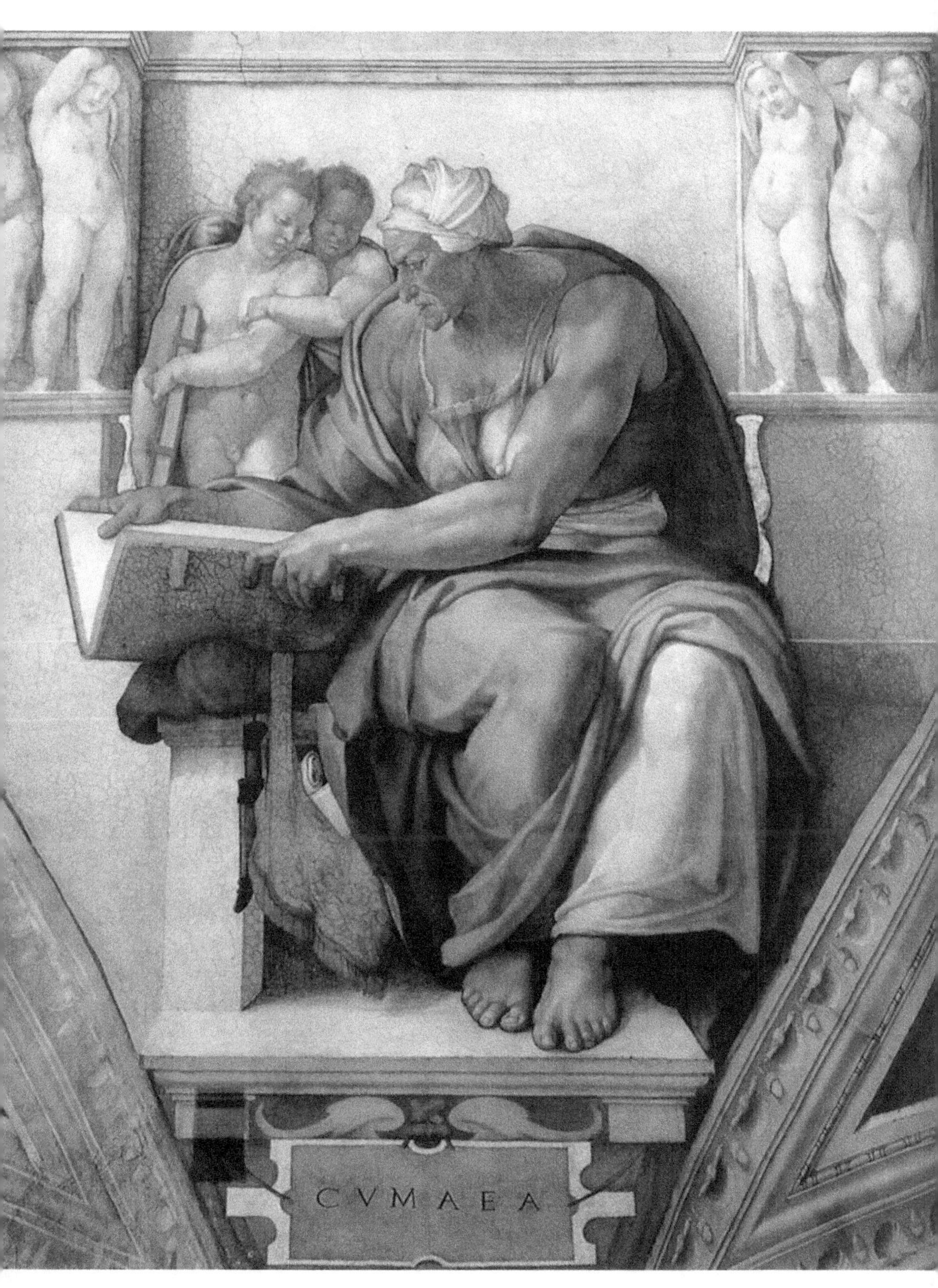

Michelangelo, Cumaean Sibyle, Sistine Chapel.

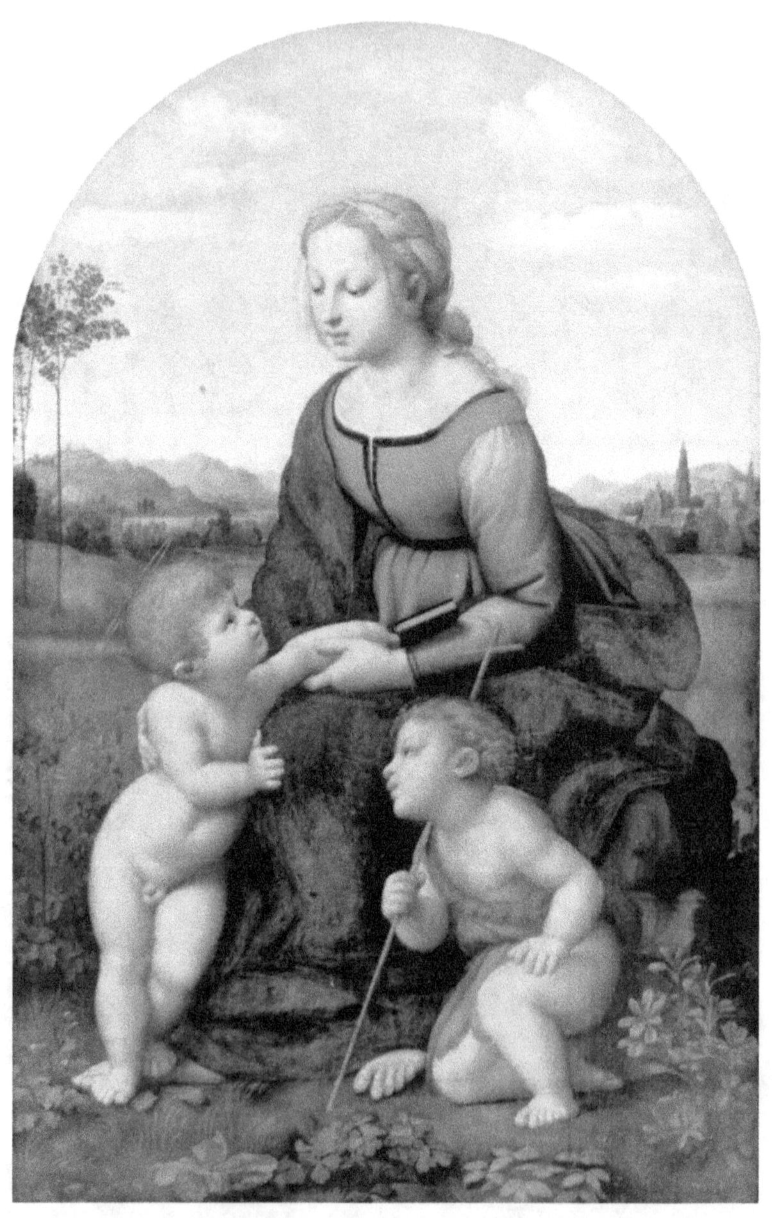

Raphael, La Belle Jardiniere, 1507, Louvre

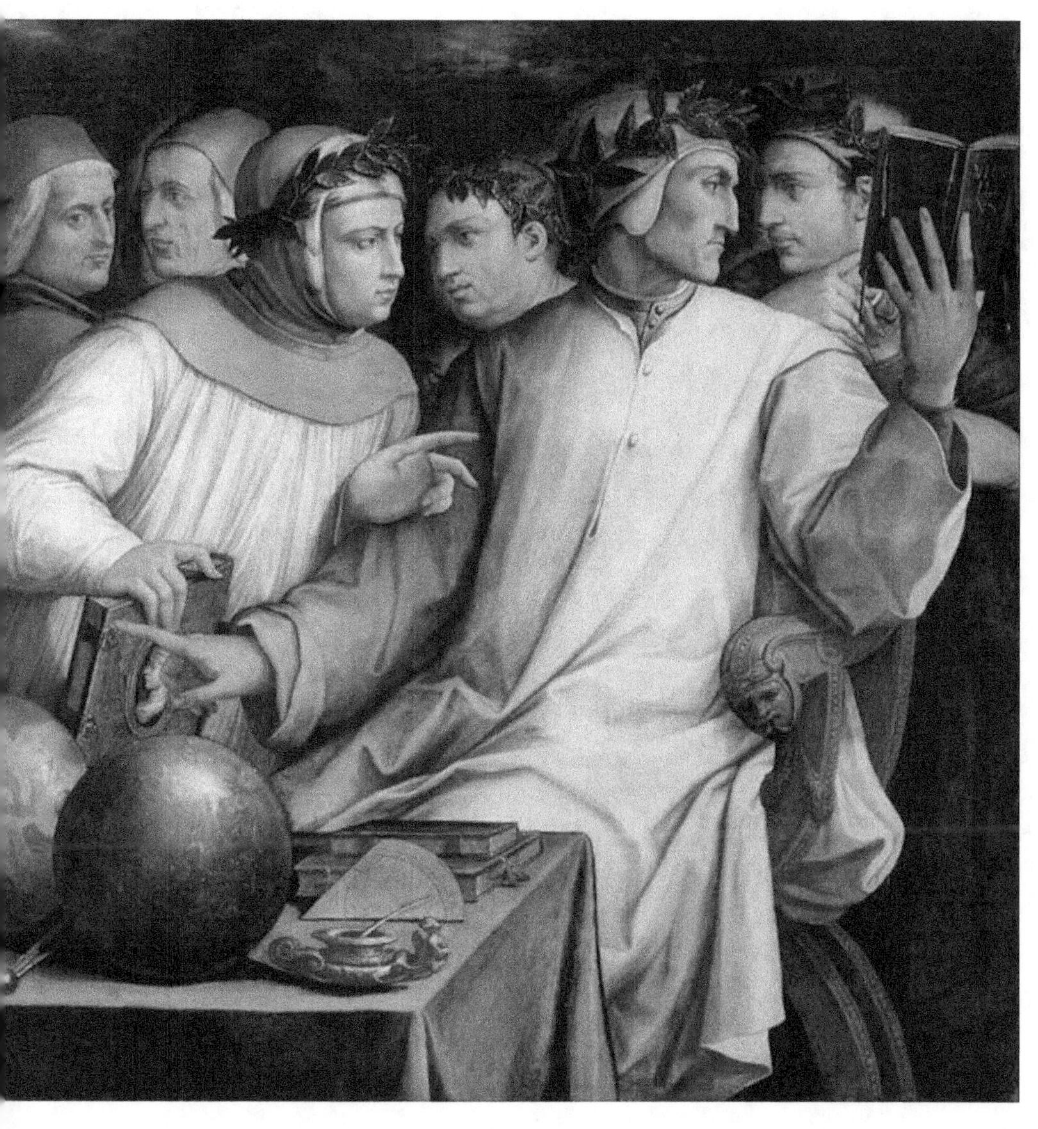

Giorgio Vasari, Six Tuscan Poets, 1544, Minneapolis

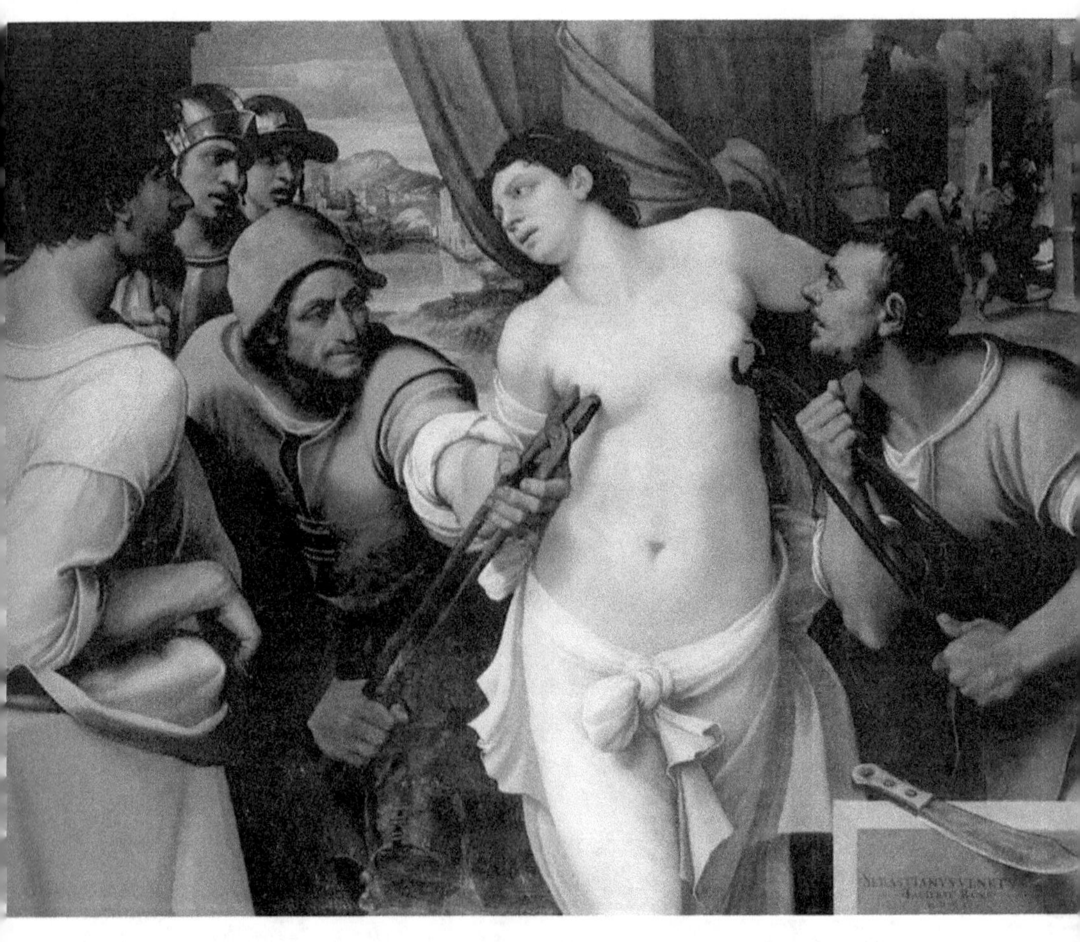

Sebastiano del Piombo, The Martyrdom of St Agatha, 1520,
Pitti Palace, Florence

NOTES

1. "The Earlier Work of Titian," *Portfolio*, October 1897.

2. According to the catalogue of 1892, this picture was formerly in the sacristy of the Escorial in Spain. It can only be by an oversight that it is therein described as "possibly painted there," since Titian never was in Spain.

3. It is especially to be noted that there is not a trace of red in the picture, save for the modest crimson waistband of the St. Catherine. Contrary to almost universal usage, it might almost be said to orthodoxy, the entire draperies of the Virgin are of one intense blue. Her veil-like head-gear is of a brownish gray, while the St. Catherine wears a golden-brown scarf, continuing the glories of her elaborately dressed hair. The audacity of the colour-scheme is only equalled by its success; no calculated effort at anything unusual being apparent. The beautiful naked *putto* who appears in the sky, arresting the progress of the shepherds, is too trivial in conception for the occasion. A similar incident is depicted in the background of the much earlier *Holy Family*, No. 4. at the National Gallery, but there the messenger angel is more appropriately and more reverently depicted as full-grown and in flowing garments.

4. Crowe and Cavalcaselle, vol. i. pp. 396, 397; *Tizian*, von H. Knackfuss, p. 55.

5. Crowe and Cavalcaselle, Appendix to vol. i. p. 448.

6. No. 1288 in the Long Gallery of the Louvre.

7. See the canvas No. 163 in the Imperial Gallery of Vienna. The want of life and of a definite personal character makes it almost repellent, notwithstanding the breadth and easy mastery of the technique. Rubens's copy of a lost or unidentified Titian, No. 845 in the same gallery, shows that he painted Isabella from life in mature middle age, and with a

truthfulness omitting no sign of over-ripeness. This portrait may very possibly have been done in 1522, when Titian appeared at the court of the Gonzagas. Its realism, even allowing for Rubens's unconscious exaggeration, might well have deterred the Gonzaga princess from being limned from life some twelve years later still.

8. Crowe and Cavalcaselle, vol. i., Appendix, p. 451.

9. The idea of painting St. Jerome by moonlight was not a new one. In the house at Venice of Andrea Odoni, the dilettante whose famous portrait by Lotto is at Hampton Court, the Anonimo (Marcantonio Michiel) saw, in 1532, "St. Jerome seated naked in a desert landscape by moonlight, by – – (sic), copied from a canvas by Zorzi da Castelfranco (Giorgione)."

10. See "The Picture Gallery of Charles I.," *The Portfolio*, January 1896, pp. 49 and 99.

11. The somewhat similar *Allegories* No. 173 and No. 187 in the Imperial Gallery at Vienna (New Catalogue, 1895), both classed as by Titian, cannot take rank as more than atelier works. Still farther from the master is the *Initiation of a Bacchante*, No. 1116 (Cat. 1891), in the Alte Pinakothek of Munich. This is a piece too cold and hard, too opaque, to have come even from his studio. It is a *pasticcio* made up in a curiously mechanical way, from the Louvre *Allegory* and the quite late *Education of Cupid* in the Borghese Gallery; the latter composition having been manifestly based by Titian himself, according to what became something like a custom in old age, upon the earlier *Allegory*.

12. A rather tiresome and lifeless portrait of Ippolito is that to be found in the picture No. 20 in the National Gallery, in which it has been assumed that his companion is his favourite painter, Sebastiano del Piombo, to whom the picture is, not without some misgivings, attributed.

13. It has been photographed under this name by Anderson of Rome.

14. In much the same position, since it hardly enjoys the celebrity to which it is entitled, is another masterpiece of portraiture from the brush of Titian, which, as belonging to his earlier middle time, should more properly have been mentioned in the first section of this monograph. This is the great *Portrait of a Man in Black*, No. 1591 in the Louvre. It shows a man of some forty years, of simple mien yet of indefinably tragic aspect; he wears moderately long hair, is clothed entirely in black, and rests his right hand on his hip, while passing the left through his belt. The dimensions of the canvas are more imposing than those of the *Jeune Homme au Gant*. No example in the Louvre, even though it competes with Madrid for the honour of possessing the greatest Titians in the world, is of finer quality than this picture. Near this – No. 1592 in the same great gallery – hangs another *Portrait of a Man in Black* by Titian, and belonging

to his middle time. The personage presented, though of high breeding, is cynical and repellent of aspect. The strong right hand rests quietly yet menacingly on a poniard, this attitude serving to give a peculiarly aggressive character to the whole conception. In the present state of this fine and striking picture the yellowness and want of transparency of the flesh-tones, both in the head and hands, gives rise to certain doubts as to the correctness of the ascription. Yet this peculiarity may well arise from injury; it would at any rate be hazardous to put forward any other name than that of Titian, to whom we must be content to leave the portrait.

15. This is the exceedingly mannered yet all the same rich and beautiful *St. Catherine, St. Roch, with a boy angel, and St. Sebastian.*

16. See Giorgione's *Adrastus and Hypsipyle (Landscape with the Soldier and the Gipsy)* of the Giovanelli Palace, the *Venus* of Dresden, the *Concert Champêtre* of the Louvre.

17. It is unnecessary in this connection to speak of the Darmstadt *Venus* invented by Crowe and Cavalcaselle, and to which as a type they so constantly refer. Giovanni Morelli has demonstrated with very general acceptance that this is only a late adaptation of the exquisite *Venus* of Dresden, which it is his greatest glory to have restored to Barbarelli and to the world.

18. *Die Galerien zu München und Dresden von Ivan Lermolieff,* p. 290.

19. Palma Vecchio, in his presentments of ripe Venetian beauty, was, we have seen, much more literal than Giorgione, more literal, too, less the poet-painter, than the young Titian. Yet in the great *Venus* of the Fitzwilliam Museum, Cambridge – not, indeed, in that of Dresden – his ideal is a higher one than Titian's in such pieces as the *Venus of Urbino* and the later *Venus,* its companion, in the Tribuna. The two Bonifazi of Verona followed Palma, giving, however, to the loveliness of their women not, indeed, a more exalted character, but a less pronounced sensuousness – an added refinement but a weaker personality. Paris Bordone took the note from Titian, but being less a great artist than a fine painter, descended a step lower in the scale. Paolo Veronese unaffectedly joys in the beauty of woman, in the sheen of fair flesh, without any under-current of deeper meaning. Tintoretto, though like his brother Venetians he delights in the rendering of the human form unveiled, is but little disquieted by the fascinating problem which now occupies us. He is by nature strangely spiritual, though he is far from indulging in any false idealisation, though he shrinks not at all from the statement of the truth as it presents itself to him. Let his famous pictures in the Anticollegio of the Doges' Palace, his *Muses* at Hampton Court, and above all that unique painted poem, *The Rescue,* in the Dresden Gallery, serve to support this

view of his art.

20. Crowe and Cavalcaselle, *Life of Titian*, vol. i. p. 420.

21. Two of these have survived in the *Roman Emperor on Horseback*, No. 257, and the similarly named picture, No. 290, at Hampton Court Palace. These panels were among the Mantua pieces purchased for Charles I. by Daniel Nys from Duke Vincenzo in 1628-29. If the Hampton Court pieces are indeed, as there appears no valid reason to doubt, two of the canvases mentioned by Vasari, we must assume that though they bore Giulio's name as *chef d'atelier*, he did little work on them himself. In the Mantuan catalogue contained in d'Arco's *Notizie* they were entered thus: – "Dieci altri quadri, dipintovi un imperatore per quadro a cavallo – opera di mano di Giulio Romano" (see *The Royal Gallery of Hampton Court*, by Ernest Law, 1898).

22. The late Charles Yriarte in a recent article, "Sabionneta la petite Athènes," published in the *Gazette des Beaux Arts*, March 1898, states that Bernardino Campi of Cremona, Giulio's subordinate at the moment, painted the Twelfth *Cæsar*, but adduces no evidence in support of this departure from the usual assumption.

23. See "The Picture Gallery of Charles I.," *The Portfolio*, October 1897, pp. 98, 99.

24. Nos. 529-540 – Catalogue of 1891 – Provincial Museum of Hanover. The dimensions are 0.19 *c.* by 0.15 *c.*

25. Of all Pordenone's exterior decorations executed in Venice nothing now remains. His only works of importance in the Venetian capital are the altar-piece in S. Giovanni Elemosinario already mentioned; the *San Lorenzo Giustiniani* altar-piece in the Accademia delle Belle Arti; the magnificent though in parts carelessly painted *Madonna del Carmelo* in the same gallery; the vast *St. Martin and St. Christopher* in the church of S. Rocco; the *Annunciation* of S. Maria degli Angeli at Murano.

26. No. 108 in the Winter Exhibition at Burlington House in 1896. By Franceschini is no doubt meant Paolo degli Franceschi, whose portrait Titian is known to have painted. He has been identified among the figures in the foreground of the *Presentation of the Virgin*.

27. See a very interesting article, "Vittore Carpaccio – La Scuola degli Albanesi," by Dr. Gustav Ludwig, in the *Archivio Storico dell' Arte* for November-December 1897.

28. A gigantic canvas of this order is, or rather was, the famous *Storm* of the Venetian Accademia, which has for many years past been dubitatively assigned to Giorgione. Vasari described it as by Palma Vecchio, stating that it was painted for the Scuola di S. Marco in the Piazza SS. Giovanni e Paolo, in rivalry with Gian Bellino(!) and

Mansueti, and referring to it in great detail and with a more fervent enthusiasm than he accords to any other Venetian picture. To the writer, judging from the parts of the original which have survived, it has long appeared that this may indeed be after all the right attribution. The ascription to Giorgione is mainly based on the romantic character of the invention, which certainly does not answer to anything that we know from the hand or brain of Palma. But then the learned men who helped Giorgione and Titian may well have helped him; and the structure of the thick-set figures in the foreground is absolutely his, as is also the sunset light on the horizon.

29. This is an arrangement analogous to that with the aid of which Tintoretto later on, in the *Crucifixion* of San Cassiano at Venice, attains to so sublime an effect. There the spears – not brandished but steadily held aloft in rigid and inflexible regularity – strangely heighten the solemn tragedy of the scene.

30. Crowe and Cavalcaselle, *Life of Titian*, vol. vi. p. 59.

31. The writer is unable to accept as a genuine design by Titian for the picture the well-known sepia drawing in the collection of the Uffizi. The composition is too clumsy in its mechanical repetition of parts, the action of the Virgin too awkward. The design looks more like an adaptation by some Bolognese eclectic.

32. This double portrait has not been preserved. According to Crowe and Cavalcaselle, the full length of Pier Luigi still exists in the Palazzo Reale at Naples (not seen by the writer).

33. The writer, who has studied in the originals all the other Titians mentioned in this monograph, has had as yet no opportunity of examining those in the Hermitage. He knows them only in the reproductions of Messrs. Braun, and in those new and admirable ones recently published by the Berlin Photographic Company.

34. This study from the life would appear to bear some such relation to the finished original as the *Innocent X.* of Velazquez at Apsley House bears to the great portrait of that Pope in the Doria Panfili collection.

35. This portrait-group belongs properly to the time a few years ahead, since it was undertaken during Titian's stay in Rome.

36. The imposing signature runs *Titianus Eques Ces. F. 1543*.

37. The type is not the nobler and more suave one seen in the *Cristo della Moneta* and the *Pilgrims of Emmaus*; it is the much less exalted one which is reproduced in the *Ecce Homo* of Madrid, and in the many repetitions and variations related to that picture, which cannot itself be accepted as an original from the hand of Titian.

38. Vasari saw a *Christ with Cleophas and Luke* by Titian, above the

door in the Salotta d'Oro, which precedes the Sala del Consiglio de' Dieci in the Doges' Palace, and states that it had been acquired by the patrician Alessandro Contarini and by him presented to the Signoria. The evidence of successive historians would appear to prove that it remained there until the close of last century. According to Crowe and Cavalcaselle the Louvre picture was a replica done for Mantua, which with the other Gonzaga pictures found its way into Charles I.'s collection, and thence, through that of Jabach, finally into the gallery of Louis XIV. At the sale of the royal collection by the Commonwealth it was appraised at £600. The picture bears the signature, unusual for this period, "Tician." There is another *Christ with the Pilgrims at Emmaus* in the collection of the Earl of Yarborough, signed "Titianus," in which, alike as to the figures, the scheme of colour, and the landscape, there are important variations. One point is of especial importance. Behind the figure of St. Luke in the Yarborough picture is a second pillar. This is not intended to appear in the Louvre picture; yet underneath the glow of the landscape there is just the shadow of such a pillar, giving evidence of a *pentimento* on the part of the master. This, so far as it goes, is evidence that the Louvre example was a revised version, and the Yarborough picture a repetition or adaptation of the first original seen by Vasari. However this may be, there can be no manner of doubt that the picture in the Long Gallery of the Louvre is an original entirely from the hand of Titian, while Lord Yarborough's picture shows nothing of his touch and little even of the manner of his studio at the time.

39. Purchased at the sale of Charles I.'s collection by Alonso de Cardenas for Philip IV. at the price of £165.

40. Crowe and Cavalcaselle, *Life of Titian*, vol. ii., Appendix (p. 502).

41. Moritz Thausing has striven in his *Wiener Kunstbriefe* to show that the coat of arms on the marble bas-relief in the *Sacred and Profane Love* is that of the well-known Nuremberg house of Imhof. This interpretation has, however, been controverted by Herz Franz Wickhoff.

42. Cesare Vecellio must have been very young at this time. The costume-book, *Degli abiti antichi e moderni*, to which he owes his chief fame, was published at Venice in 1590.

43. "Das Tizianbildniss der königlichen Galerie zu Cassel," *Jahrbuch der königlich-preussischen Kunstsammlungen*, Funfzehnter Band, III. Heft.

44. See the *Francesco Maria, Duke of Urbino* at the Uffizi; also, for the modish headpiece, the *Ippolito de' Medici* at the Pitti.

45. A number of fine portraits must of necessity be passed over in these remarks. The superb if not very well-preserved *Antonio Portia*, within the last few years added to the Brera, dates back a good many years from this time. Then we have, among other things, the *Benedetto*

Varchi and the *Fabrizio Salvaresio* of the Imperial Museum at Vienna – the latter bearing the date 1558. The writer is unable to accept as a genuine Titian the interesting but rather matter-of-fact *Portrait of a Lady in Mourning*, No. 174 in the Dresden Gallery. The master never painted with such a lack of charm and distinction. Very doubtful, but difficult to judge in its present state, is the *Portrait of a Lady with a Vase*, No. 173 in the same collection. Morelli accepts as a genuine example of the master the *Portrait of a Lady in a Red Dress* also in the Dresden Gallery, where it bears the number 176. If the picture is his, as the technical execution would lead the observer to believe, it constitutes in its stiffness and unambitious *naïveté* a curious exception in his long series of portraits.

46. It is impossible to discuss here the atelier repetitions in the collections of the National Gallery and Lord Wemyss respectively, or the numerous copies to be found in other places.

47. For the full text of the marriage contract see Giovanni Morelli, *Die Galerien zu München und Dresden*, pp. 300-302.

48. Joshua Reynolds, who saw it during his tour in Italy, says: "It is so dark a picture that, at first casting my eyes on it, I thought there was a black curtain before it."

49. Crowe and Cavalcaselle, vol. ii. p. 272.

50. They were, with the *Rape of Europa*, among the so-called "light pieces" presented to Prince Charles by Philip IV., and packed for transmission to England. On the collapse of the marriage negotiations they were, however, kept back. Later on Philip V. presented them to the Marquis de Grammont. They subsequently formed part of the Orleans Gallery, and were acquired at the great sale in London by the Duke of Bridgewater for £2500 apiece.

51. This great piece is painted on a canvas of peculiarly coarse grain, with a well-defined lozenge pattern. It was once owned by Van Dyck, at the sale of whose possessions, in 1556, a good number of years after his death, it was acquired by Algernon Percy, Earl of Northumberland. In 1873 it was in the exhibition of Old Masters at the Royal Academy.

52. The best repetition of this Hermitage *Magdalen* is that in the Naples Museum; another was formerly in the Ashburton Collection, and yet another is in the Durazzo Gallery at Genoa. The similar, but not identical, picture in the Yarborough Collection is anything but "cold in tone," as Crowe and Cavalcaselle call it. It is, on the contrary, rich in colour, but as to the head of the saint, much less attractive than the original.

53. This picture was presented by Philip IV. to Prince Charles of England, and was, at the sale of his collection, acquired by Jabach for

£600, and from him bought by Cardinal Mazarin, whose heirs sold it to Louis XIV. The Cardinal thus possessed the two finest representations of the *Jupiter and Antiope* legend – that by Correggio (also now in the Louvre) and the Titian. It was to these pictures especially that his touching farewell was addressed a few hours before his death.

54. See Crowe and Cavalcaselle, vol. ii., Appendix, p. 340.

55. See as to the vicissitudes through which the picture has passed an article, "Les Restaurations du tableau du Titien, *Jupiter et Antiope*" by Fernand Engerand, in the *Chronique des Arts* of 7th May 1898.

56. This picture came to England with the Orleans Gallery, and was until lately at Cobham Hall in the collection of the Earl of Darnley. It has now passed into that of Mrs J.L. Gardner of Boston, U.S. It is represented in the Prado Gallery by Rubens's superb copy. A Venetian copy on a very small scale exists in the Wallace Collection.

57. A very clever adaptation of this work is No. 490 in the Prado Gallery under the name of the master. It is remarkable for the contrast between the moonlight which irradiates the Christ and the artificial light supplied by the lantern carried by one of the soldiers.

58. This picture is mentioned in the list of 1574 furnished by Titian to Secretary Antonio Perez. A *Perseus and Andromeda* by, or attributed to, Titian was in the Orleans Gallery. Is this the canvas now in the Wallace Collection, but not as yet publicly exhibited there? This last piece was undoubtedly produced in the *entourage* and with the assistance of Titian, and it corresponds perfectly to Vasari's description of the *Deliverance of Andromeda*. It has the loose easy touch of the late time, but obscured as it at present is by dirt and successive coats of now discoloured varnish, no more definite opinion with regard to its merits can be given. No. 135 in the Hermitage is a canvas identical in subject and dimensions with this last-named picture. It was once attributed to Tintoretto, but is now put down to the school of Titian.

59. Somewhat earlier in the order of the late works should come in, if we may venture to judge from the technique of a work that is practically a ruin, the *Adam and Eve* of the Prado, in which, for the usual serpent with the human head of the feminine type, Titian has substituted as tempter an insignificant *amorino*. Far more enjoyable than this original in its present state is the magnificent copy, with slight yet marked variations, left behind by Rubens. This is also to be found in the Prado. A drawing by the great Antwerper from Titian's picture is in the Louvre. This is more markedly Flemish in aspect than the painted canvas, and lacks the foolish little Love.

60. Formerly in the collection of the Earl of Dudley, upon the sale of

which it was acquired by Mr. Ludwig Mond. It was in the Venetian exhibition at the New Gallery. There is an engraving of it by Pieter de Jode, jun.

61. This is No. 186 in the catalogue of 1895. An etching of the picture appeared with an article "Les Écoles d'Italie au Musée de Vienne," from the pen of Herr Franz Wickhoff, in the *Gazette des Beaux Arts* for February 1893. It was badly engraved for the Teniers Gallery by Lissebetius.

62. Now in the Accademia delle Belle Arti of Venice.

63. It was the intention of the writer to add to this monograph a short chapter on the drawings of Titian. The subject is, however, far too vast for such summary treatment, and its discussion must therefore be postponed. Leaving out of the question the very numerous drawings by Domenico Campagnola which Morelli has once for all separated from those of the greater master, and those also which, while belonging to the same class and period, are neither Titian's nor even Campagnola's, a few of the genuine landscapes may be just lightly touched upon. The beautiful early landscape with a battlemented castle, now or lately in the possession of Mr. T.W. Russell (reproduction in the British Museum marked 1879-5-10-224) is in the opinion of the writer a genuine Titian. *The Vision of St. Eustace*, reproduced in the first section of this monograph ("The Earlier Work of Titian") from the original in the British Museum, is a noble and pathetic example of the earlier manner. Perhaps the most beautiful of the landscape drawings still preserving something of the Giorgionesque aroma is that with the enigmatic female figure, entirely nude but with the head veiled, and the shepherds sheltering from the noonday sun, which is in the great collection at Chatsworth (No. 318 in Venetian Exhibition at New Gallery). Later than this is the fine landscape in the same collection with a riderless horse crossing a stream (No. 867 in Venetian Exhibition at New Gallery). The well-known *St. Jerome* here given (British Museum) is ascribed by no less an authority than Giovanni Morelli to the master, but the poor quality of the little round trees, and of the background generally, is calculated to give pause to the student. A good example of the later style, in which the technique is more that of the painter and less that of the draughtsman, is the so-called *Landscape with the Pedlar* at Chatsworth. But, faded though it is, the finest extant drawing of the later period is that here (p. 78) for the first time reproduced by the kind permission of the owner, Professor Legros, who had the great good fortune and good taste to discover it in a London bookshop. There can be no doubt that this ought to be in the Print Room at the British Museum. A good instance, on the other hand, of a drawing which cannot without demur be left to Titian, though it is a good deal too late in style for Domenico

Campagnola, and moreover, much too fine and sincere for that clever, facile adapter of other people's work, is the beautiful pastoral in the Albertina at Vienna (B. 283), with the shepherd piping as he leads his flock homewards.

ARTS, PAINTING, SCULPTURE

The Art of Andy Goldsworthy
Andy Goldsworthy: Touching Nature
Andy Goldsworthy in Close-Up
Andy Goldsworthy: Pocket Guide
Andy Goldsworthy In America
Land Art: A Complete Guide
The Art of Richard Long
Richard Long: Pocket Guide
Land Art In the UK
Land Art in Close-Up
Land Art In the U.S.A.
Land Art: Pocket Guide
Installation Art in Close-Up
Minimal Art and Artists In the 1960s and After
Colourfield Painting
Land Art DVD, TV documentary
Andy Goldsworthy DVD, TV documentary
The Erotic Object: Sexuality in Sculpture From Prehistory to the Present Day
Sex in Art: Pornography and Pleasure in Painting and Sculpture
Postwar Art
Sacred Gardens: The Garden in Myth, Religion and Art
Glorification: Religious Abstraction in Renaissance and 20th Century Art
Early Netherlandish Painting
Leonardo da Vinci
Piero della Francesca
Giovanni Bellini
Fra Angelico: Art and Religion in the Renaissance
Mark Rothko: The Art of Transcendence
Frank Stella: American Abstract Artist
Jasper Johns
Brice Marden
Alison Wilding: The Embrace of Sculpture
Vincent van Gogh: Visionary Landscapes
Eric Gill: Nuptials of God
Constantin Brancusi: Sculpting the Essence of Things
Max Beckmann
Caravaggio
Gustave Moreau
Egon Schiele: Sex and Death In Purple Stockings
Delizioso Fotografico Fervore: Works In Process 1
Sacro Cuore: Works In Process 2
The Light Eternal: J.M.W. Turner
The Madonna Glorified: Karen Arthurs

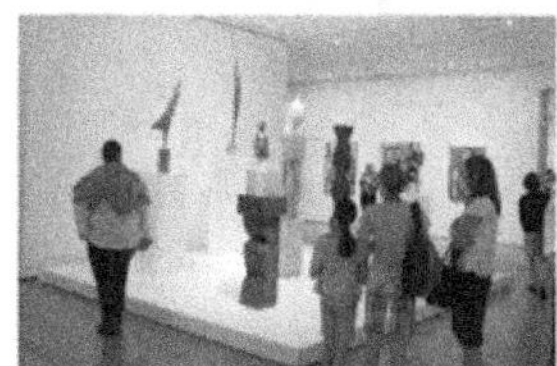
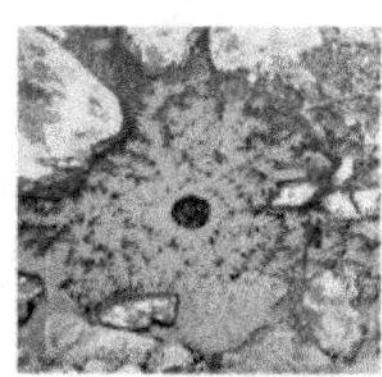
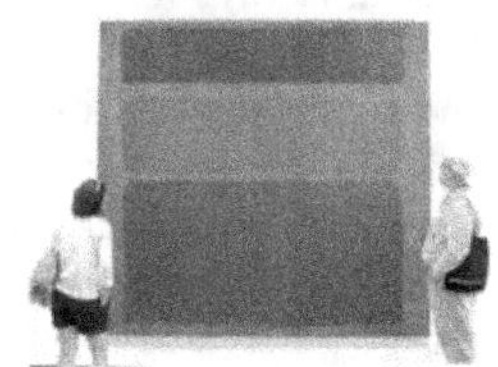
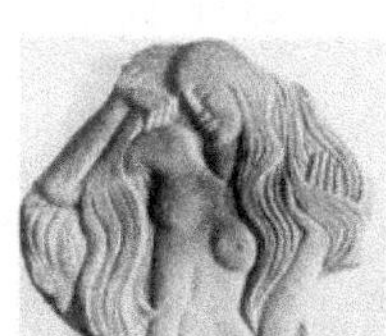
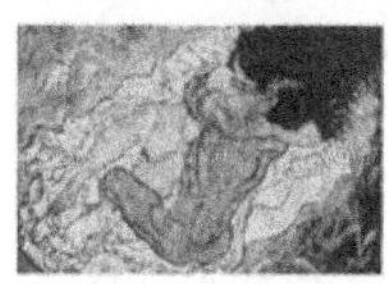
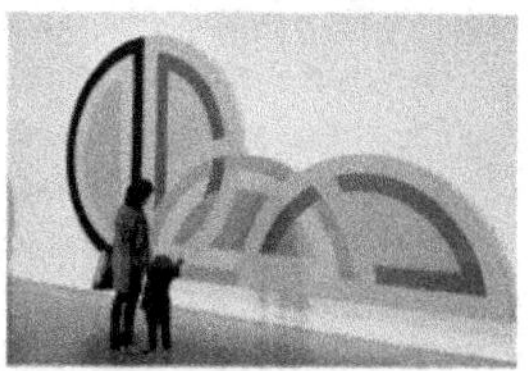
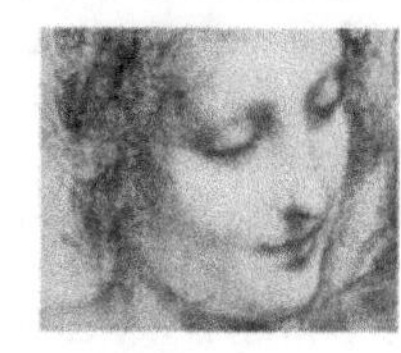
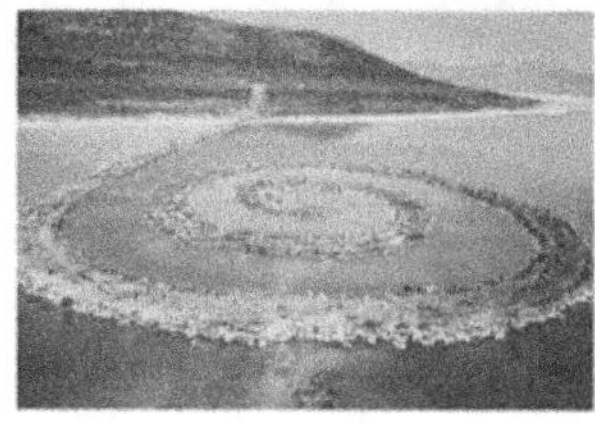

LITERATURE

J.R.R. Tolkien: The Books, The Films, The Whole Cultural Phenomenon
J.R.R. Tolkien: Pocket Guide
Tolkien's Heroic Quest
The *Earthsea* Books of Ursula Le Guin
Beauties, Beasts and Enchantment: Classic French Fairy Tales
German Popular Stories by the Brothers Grimm
Philip Pullman and *His Dark Materials*
Sexing Hardy: Thomas Hardy and Feminism
Thomas Hardy's *Tess of the d'Urbervilles* 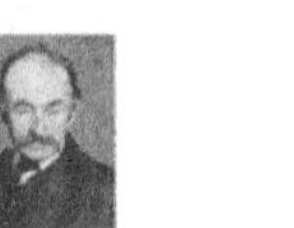 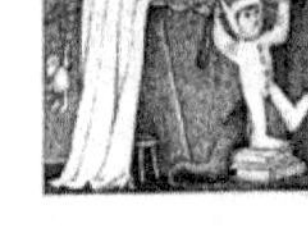
Thomas Hardy's *Jude the Obscure*
Thomas Hardy: The Tragic Novels
Love and Tragedy: Thomas Hardy
The Poetry of Landscape in Hardy
Wessex Revisited: Thomas Hardy and John Cowper Powys
Wolfgang Iser: Essays and Interviews 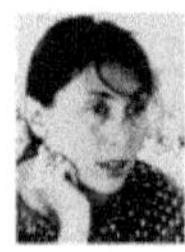
Petrarch, Dante and the Troubadours
Maurice Sendak and the Art of Children's Book Illustration
Andrea Dworkin 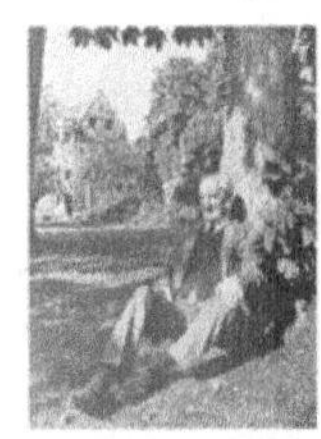
Cixous, Irigaray, Kristeva: The *Jouissance* of French Feminism
Julia Kristeva: Art, Love, Melancholy, Philosophy, Semiotics and Psychoanalysis
Hélene Cixous I Love You: The *Jouissance* of Writing
Luce Irigaray: Lips, Kissing, and the Politics of Sexual Difference
Peter Redgrove: Here Comes the Flood
Peter Redgrove: Sex-Magic-Poetry-Cornwall
Lawrence Durrell: Between Love and Death, East and West 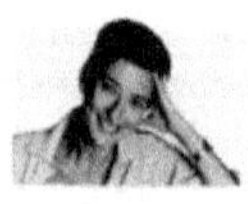
Love, Culture & Poetry: Lawrence Durrell
Cavafy: Anatomy of a Soul
German Romantic Poetry: Goethe, Novalis, Heine, Hölderlin
Feminism and Shakespeare 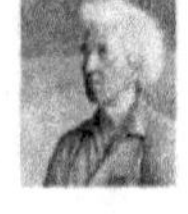
Shakespeare: Love, Poetry & Magic
The Passion of D.H. Lawrence 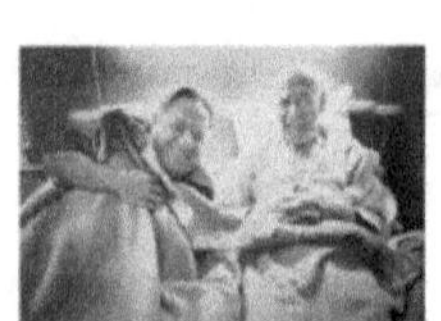
D.H. Lawrence: Symbolic Landscapes
D.H. Lawrence: Infinite Sensual Violence
Rimbaud: Arthur Rimbaud and the Magic of Poetry
The Ecstasies of John Cowper Powys
Sensualism and Mythology: The Wessex Novels of John Cowper Powys
Amorous Life: John Cowper Powys and the Manifestation of Affectivity (H.W. Fawkner)
Postmodern Powys: New Essays on John Cowper Powys (Joe Boulter)
Rethinking Powys: Critical Essays on John Cowper Powys
Paul Bowles & Bernardo Bertolucci
Rainer Maria Rilke
Joseph Conrad: *Heart of Darkness* 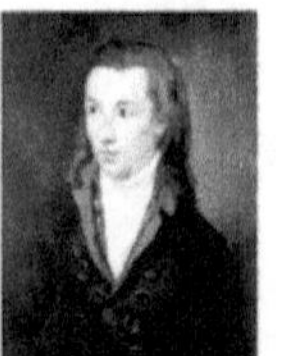
In the Dim Void: Samuel Beckett
Samuel Beckett Goes into the Silence
André Gide: Fiction and Fervour
Jackie Collins and the Blockbuster Novel
Blinded By Her Light: The Love-Poetry of Robert Graves
The Passion of Colours: Travels In Mediterranean Lands
Poetic Forms

POETRY

Ursula Le Guin: Walking In Cornwall
Peter Redgrove: Here Comes The Flood
Peter Redgrove: Sex-Magic-Poetry-Cornwall
Dante: Selections From the Vita Nuova
Petrarch, Dante and the Troubadours
William Shakespeare: Sonnets
William Shakespeare: Complete Poems
Blinded By Her Light: The Love-Poetry of Robert Graves
Emily Dickinson: Selected Poems
Emily Brontë: Poems
Thomas Hardy: Selected Poems
Percy Bysshe Shelley: Poems
John Keats: Selected Poems
Joh n Keats: Poems of 1820
D.H. Lawrence: Selected Poems
Edmund Spenser: Poems
Edmund Spenser: Amoretti
John Donne: Poems
Henry Vaughan: Poems
Sir Thomas Wyatt: Poems
Robert Herrick: Selected Poems
Rilke: Space, Essence and Angels in the Poetry of Rainer Maria Rilke
Rainer Maria Rilke: Selected Poems
Friedrich Hölderlin: Selected Poems
Arseny Tarkovsky: Selected Poems
Arthur Rimbaud: Selected Poems
Arthur Rimbaud: A Season in Hell
Arthur Rimbaud and the Magic of Poetry
Novalis: Hymns To the Night
German Romantic Poetry
Paul Verlaine: Selected Poems
Elizaethan Sonnet Cycles
D.J. Enright: By-Blows
Jeremy Reed: Brigitte's Blue Heart
Jeremy Reed: Claudia Schiffer's Red Shoes
Gorgeous Little Orpheus
Radiance: New Poems
Crescent Moon Book of Nature Poetry
Crescent Moon Book of Love Poetry
Crescent Moon Book of Mystical Poetry
Crescent Moon Book of Elizabethan Love Poetry
Crescent Moon Book of Metaphysical Poetry
Crescent Moon Book of Romantic Poetry
Pagan America: New American Poetry

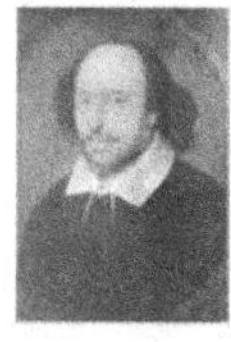
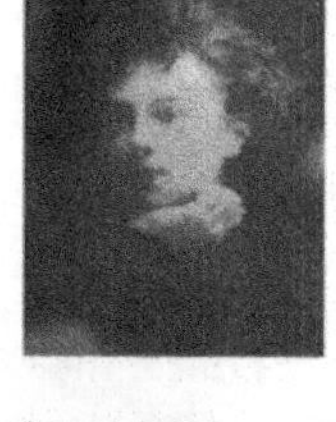
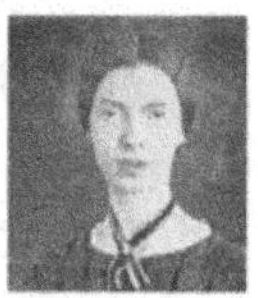
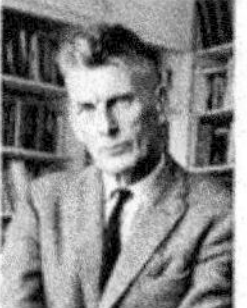
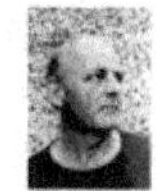
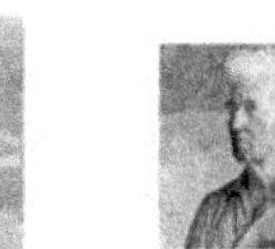
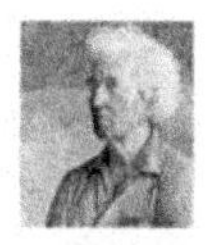
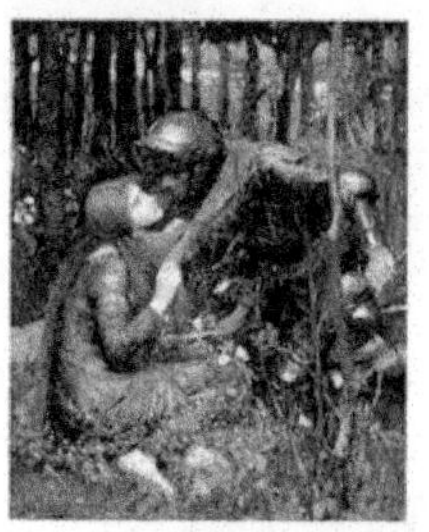
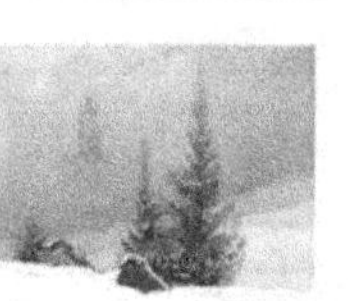
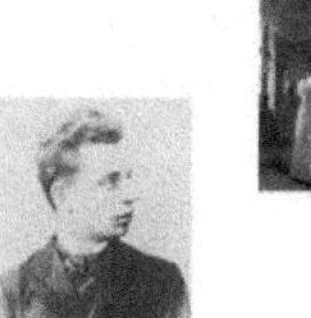
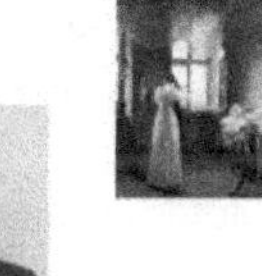
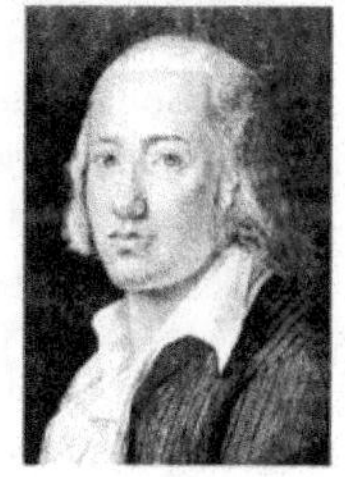
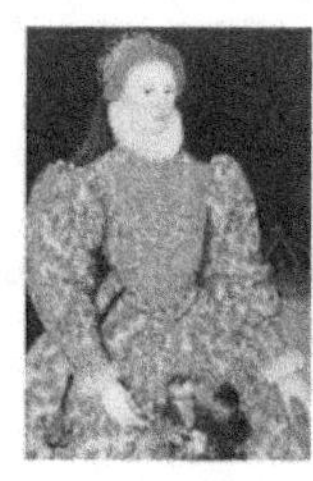

MEDIA, CINEMA, FEMINISM and CULTURAL STUDIES

J.R.R. Tolkien: The Books, The Films, The Whole Cultural Phenomenon
J.R.R. Tolkien: Pocket Guide
The *Lord of the Rings* Movies: Pocket Guide
The Cinema of Hayao Miyazaki
Hayao Miyazaki: *Princess Mononoke*: Pocket Movie Guide
Hayao Miyazaki: *Spirited Away*: Pocket Movie Guide
Tim Burton : Hallowe'en For Hollywood
Ken Russell
Ken Russell: *Tommy*: Pocket Movie Guide
The Ghost Dance: The Origins of Religion
The Peyote Cult

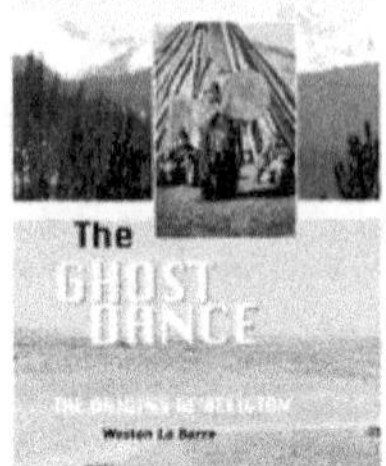

Cixous, Irigaray, Kristeva: The *Jouissance* of French Feminism
Julia Kristeva: Art, Love, Melancholy, Philosophy, Semiotics and Psychoanalysis
Luce Irigaray: Lips, Kissing, and the Politics of Sexual Difference
Hélene Cixous I Love You: The *Jouissance* of Writing
Andrea Dworkin
'Cosmo Woman': The World of Women's Magazines
Women in Pop Music
HomeGround: The Kate Bush Anthology
Discovering the Goddess (Geoffrey Ashe)
The Poetry of Cinema

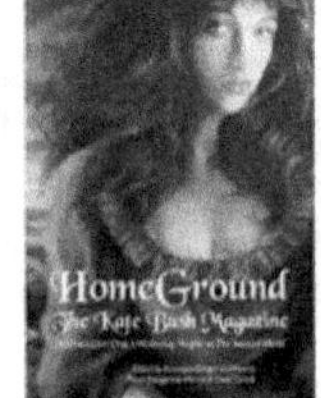

The Sacred Cinema of Andrei Tarkovsky
Andrei Tarkovsky: Pocket Guide
Andrei Tarkovsky: *Mirror*: Pocket Movie Guide
Andrei Tarkovsky: *The Sacrifice*: Pocket Movie Guide
Walerian Borowczyk: Cinema of Erotic Dreams
Jean-Luc Godard: The Passion of Cinema
Jean-Luc Godard: *Hail Mary*: Pocket Movie Guide

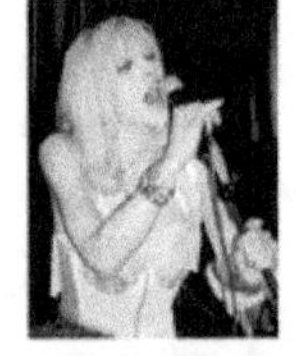

Jean-Luc Godard: *Contempt*: Pocket Movie Guide
Jean-Luc Godard: *Pierrot le Fou*: Pocket Movie Guide
John Hughes and Eighties Cinema
Ferris Bueller's Day Off: Pocket Movie Guide
Jean-Luc Godard: Pocket Guide
The Cinema of Richard Linklater

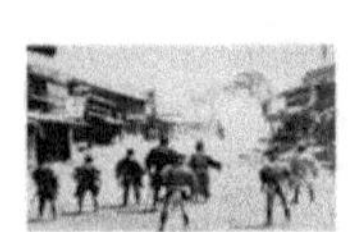

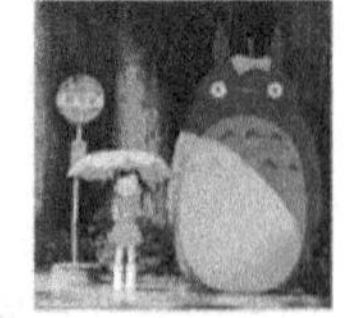

Liv Tyler: Star In Ascendance
Blade Runner and the Films of Philip K. Dick
Paul Bowles and Bernardo Bertolucci
Media Hell: Radio, TV and the Press
An Open Letter to the BBC

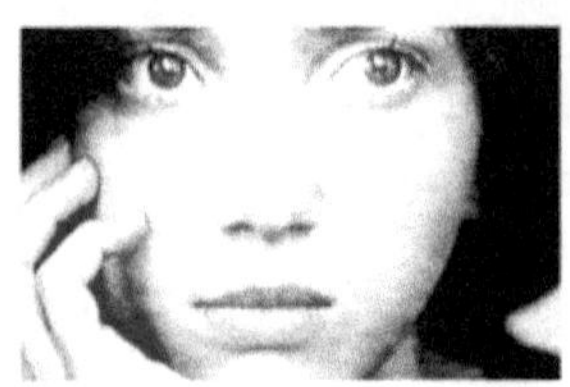

Detonation Britain: Nuclear War in the UK
Feminism and Shakespeare
Wild Zones: Pornography, Art and Feminism
Sex in Art: Pornography and Pleasure in Painting and Sculpture
Sexing Hardy: Thomas Hardy and Feminism

The Light Eternal is a model monograph, an exemplary job. The subject matter of the book is beautifully organised and dead on beam. (Lawrence Durrell)
It is amazing for me to see my work treated with such passion and respect. (Andrea Dworkin)

CRESCENT MOON PUBLISHING
P.O. Box 1312, Maidstone, Kent, ME14 5XU, Great Britain. www.crmoon.com

cresmopub@yahoo.co.uk   www.crescentmoon.org.uk